THE
HAPPINESS
EQUATION

The Surprising Economics of
Our Most Valuable Asset

Nick Powdthavee

ICON BOOKS

First published in the UK in 2010 by Icon Books Ltd

This edition published in the UK in 2011 by
Icon Books Ltd, Omnibus Business Centre,
39–41 North Road, London N7 9DP
email: info@iconbooks.co.uk
www.iconbooks.co.uk

Sold in the UK, Europe, South Africa and Asia
by Faber & Faber Ltd, Bloomsbury House,
74–77 Great Russell Street,
London WC1B 3DA or their agents

Distributed in the UK, Europe, South Africa and Asia
by TBS Ltd, TBS Distribution Centre, Colchester Road,
Frating Green, Colchester CO7 7DW

Published in Australia in 2011 by
Allen & Unwin Pty Ltd, PO Box 8500,
83 Alexander Street, Crows Nest, NSW 2065

Published in the USA in 2011 by Totem Books
Inquiries to: Icon Books Ltd., Omnibus Business Centre,
39–41 North Road, London N7 9DP, UK

Distributed to the trade in the USA
by Consortium Book Sales & Distribution
The Keg House, 34 Thirteenth Avenue NE, Suite 101
Minneapolis, Minnesota 55413-1007

Distributed in Canada by Penguin Books Canada,
90 Eglinton Avenue East, Suite 700,
Toronto, Ontario M4P 2YE

ISBN: 978-184831-246-3

Typeset in Minion by Marie Doherty

Printed and bound in the UK by
Clays Ltd, St Ives plc

CONTENTS

About the Author

Dr Nattavudh (Nick) Powdthavee is a behavioural economist at Nanyang Technological University, Singapore. Discussions of his work on the economics of happiness have appeared in over 50 major international newspapers in the past five years, including the *New York Times*, *Financial Times* and the *Guardian*, as well as on TV, including Channel 5 News and *The Wright Stuff*. He is originally from Thailand.

To Andrew, for telling me, all those years ago,
that it's okay to do the things other people don't do.

Also to Nateecha, for telling me, some years later,
that it's okay to do the things other people do, too.

Happiness is not having what you want,
but wanting what you have.

Rabbi Hyman Schachtel

CHAPTER 1

THE PURSUIT

Most of us go through life believing we know exactly what we need to make us happy. For the most part, we believe that all we ever need is to have someone we love loving us back. Or it's a combination of more money, a good job, a stable marriage and perfect health. Sometimes it's the little things in life, like a day off work; a clear blue sky on an autumn afternoon; a nice cup of cool mochaccino on a hot day; an hour-long foot rub; a day spent laughing with friends and family; 45 minutes of uninterrupted sex with our partner, and the energy to last for the best part of it.

But unfortunately – in the words of Mick Jagger and Keith Richards – we can't always get what we want. At least, we can't always get what we want all the time. A day off work every so often sounds like a good idea until, of course, we realise that we will become a little poorer because of it. And that's no good because, according to the abstract idea we have in our heads of what makes a good life, money matters a lot. Okay then, in that case, we'll put in more hours at work. But wait. That will also mean less time to be spent with friends and family, and that doesn't seem so good either.

So what do we do, then? What do we do when our lives are a series of trade-offs between different combinations of 'what ifs'? What do we do when there is an endless horizon of time and resource constraints constantly telling us that whatever we do, we can't possibly have it all? Well, according to economists, who are supposedly experts on decision-making, what usually happens is that we try to do the best we can with our choices.

We gather all necessary information about our options. We engage in rationalisation and mental calculations. We quietly argue and debate within ourselves over the potential impacts of each individual decision on our happiness. We cross-refer them to the rule-book of 'All the things that make *me* happy', put each possibility into an order of preference, and then, subject to both time and resource constraints, choose the best combination of bundles that we know would optimise our well-being.

Easy.

Bounded rationality

But of course, if that were true – if we always chose the best possible combination of options according to stable preference functions and the constraints facing them – then the way we led our lives would literally be disappointment-free. Whatever decisions we made, we would know exactly well in advance what we were getting ourselves into. After all, our rationality would have already done the homework for us: we would be getting the greatest reward at the lowest cost.

How could we possibly not be happy with that?

The reality, however, is that our lives are too often filled with disappointing and regrettable decisions, whether big or small. The holiday we went on last summer; that antique car we bought; or even the job or college degrees we picked. The following anecdotal evidence from a chance meeting between two economists and a dentist makes it all too clear.[1]

Two economics professors and friends, John Bennett and Chuck Blackorby, were attending an economics conference. On the first evening, they met a dentist at the hotel bar who was at an annual conference for dentists just next door to them. After a brief introduction and a couple of drinks, Chuck, who was known for his sometimes brash and direct manner, decided to ask the dentist, by then a little tipsy, a somewhat personal question.

'So, tell me, are you very happy being a dentist?'

'Happy? I'm miserable as a dentist', replied the man.

Chuck smiled to himself. 'What? If you're so unhappy, why on earth did you choose to become a dentist in the first place?'

'I didn't choose to become a dentist.' The man took another swig of his drink before delivering the final hammer blow. 'It's that stupid kid eighteen years ago that chose to become a dentist. Not me.'

And even when we're not too disappointed; when we actually think we're fairly satisfied with the choices we made, sometimes there's just no way for us to know for certain whether or not we would have been happier if we'd gone with the alternatives. Take having children, for example. For most parents, a natural and genuine response to the question, 'Would you be happier without children?' would be a screaming 'No!' However, there's no real way of knowing precisely what life would have been like if these parents had decided not to have their little David or Sarah – simply because the childless alternative didn't take place for them. The same argument holds true for partners who choose not to become parents.

One of the main reasons why we aren't always able to choose the best options for ourselves is that our rationality is often bounded by the amount of information it possesses, the cognitive limitations of our brains,[2] and the finite amount of time we have to make a decision.[3] According to the so-called 'bounded rationality' concept, we human beings are only partly rational – and downright irrational in the remaining part of our actions.

While economists believe that all human beings are approximately *Homo economicus* (economic man), rational and broadly self-interested by nature, the reality is that we are just as likely, if not more likely, to let emotions overrule rationality and completely dictate the way we behave.

That we are not wholly rational is shown by studies that have identified two distinct sides to our brains: one that is rational – controlled, slow, deliberative and deductive; and one that is emotional – automatic, rapid, associative and affective.[4] The mesh between the two is extremely complex, and one does not always dominate the other. And while economic theories of decision-making have tended to emphasise the operation of the rational side of our brain in guiding choice behaviour, it's often the case that, when making decisions under pressure or under conditions where information is incomplete or overly complex, we tend to rely on simplifying heuristics or 'gut feelings' rather than extensive algorithmic processing.[5] These 'rules of thumb' are far from perfect, and it's precisely why we sometimes spend too much money on food when we go grocery shopping with an empty stomach,[6] or find it increasingly difficult to walk away from a bus stop the longer we have been waiting for a bus to come – even if it would have been a lot quicker to walk than to wait for that damn bus to arrive.[7]

The adaptive unconscious and past experiences

But maybe it's not always such a bad thing to trust our emotions. Research carried out by psychology professor Timothy Wilson suggests that, in situations where we have had a lot of experience, decisions made without thinking (those made on impulses and gut feelings) can often lead to better and happier outcomes than if they had been made under a strict rule of optimisation, simply because this is when the emotional part of our brain works best at detecting that something is out of the ordinary – even if we may not know ourselves *what* that something is at the time – and alerts us in the form of emotional alarm bells such as sweaty palms and butterflies in our stomach.[8] And it's in these scenarios that practice really makes perfect. It's also where thinking too much about our past experiences can actually hurt rather than help us.

The question is: Why?

One reason. According to psychologist and Nobel laureate Daniel Kahneman, the cognitive part of our brain tends to suffer from what he called the 'peak-end' effect, which is the tendency to judge past experiences – both pleasant and unpleasant – almost entirely on how they were at their peak and how they ended.[9]

Kahneman and his colleagues illustrated the core concept of the peak-end theory in a series of experiments, most notably that involving hospital patients and the very painful colonoscopy procedure.[10] While undergoing a colonoscopy, the patients reported their level of discomfort every 60 seconds throughout the procedure. Afterwards, the patients were asked to remember how unpleasant the procedure was, using several different scales including a ten-point scale, and also about the relative unpleasantness of the colonoscopy compared to other unpleasant experiences such as stubbing a toe, or an average visit to the dentist. What Kahneman and his colleagues found was astonishing. While there was almost zero correlation between the duration of the colonoscopies that different patients experienced and the global rating of the procedure, the relationship between the peak-end average (the average of the peaks and how the patients felt at the end of the procedure) and the global rating of the procedure was simply undeniable. In other words, we are more likely to remember our experience of a colonoscopy as being awful if the peaks of unpleasantness were very high or if it ended awfully for us, than if the entire procedure itself took a long time to finish. What matters is not the duration of an experience; we hardly ever think about it when we try to recall and judge how happy or unhappy we were in the past. It's how we were feeling at the peaks and at the end of our experience that count the most.

What about frequency? Surely having experienced something often can teach us to repeat only the things that we remember with pleasure and fondness, and avoid those that we remember with embarrassment and regret? The trouble is, according to Harvard psychologist Daniel Gilbert, we are just not very good at remembering them correctly. He illustrates his point by prompting the readers of his book – *Stumbling on Happiness* – to think about where they were, whom they were with, and what they were doing when they first heard the news about the 9/11 attacks in 2001.[11] Okay, that sounds easy enough. Closing my eyes, I can still remember that I was standing at one of the check-in counters at London Heathrow airport, trying to get on the evening flight to Bangkok. Sitting behind the Finnair counter was a man in his late 50s who, as I recall, spoke with a very thick Glaswegian accent.

'So you're off to Thailand then, eh? Ah, what a beautiful country! Lovely food, gorgeous beaches, very pretty women!' His eyes twinkled as he said this.

I smiled politely, acknowledging his appreciation of my country of birth. I knew he was just trying to be friendly in what seemed to be a surprisingly empty airport on a Tuesday afternoon.

'Okay, sir. Here's your boarding pass. Have a nice flight … Oh, and have you heard? Two planes hit the World Trade Center not half an hour ago. Probably a terrorist attack. But since you're flying to Finland first, I'm sure you'll be just fine.' He ended with a beam while I stood there, rigid as a board.

Like me, most people will be able to remember in fine detail what they were doing when they first heard the news. But, Gilbert added – would the same people also remember precisely where they were, whom they were with, and what they were doing on the morning of 10 September 2001, one day before the attacks?

I personally couldn't, of course. And I'm confident enough to bet that not many people could either – a fact that is also true for most Americans.

The main reason why it's relatively easier for us to recall the exact details of 11 September 2001, but nearly impossible to remember what happened a day earlier, is because momentous events like the 9/11 attacks do not happen frequently in our lifetime. While 11 September 2001 defied our every sense of normality, 10 September, by contrast, was like almost any other day. And unless we religiously keep a diary of everything that ever happened in our lives, any other day is nothing more than a blob in our memory bank.

Daniel Gilbert's message is clear: it is the infrequent and unusual experiences that are most memorable. These are the ones that stick like glue to the clipboard of our memory cortex. Not the other way round.

Conventional wisdom and imagination

There are two lessons we can draw at this stage. The first is that, in situations where we have had a lot of experience, it's perhaps better to trust our instincts when it comes to making a decision. And the second lesson, related to the first, is that it seems important not to rely completely on emotions in situations where we have had little or no prior experience. The explanation is simple: in these circumstances, the emotional part of our brain will not have had enough chances to adapt and learn from our past experiences, which will inevitably make it impossible for it to distinguish which decision is better for us.[12]

That sounds perfectly reasonable. All we need to do now is follow any great professional's advice and just practise, practise, practise. Then afterwards, we can sit back in situations where we have had a lot of these experiences and just make snap decisions without having to think too much about the best outcomes.

Two problems, though. First, how do we know when we have had enough practice doing something? How do we know when we can let the rational brain take a back seat and the emotional brain do all the work? Will 10,000 hours of doing something repetitively be enough?[13] Or will it take a lifetime of experience? Second, what about other, more novel situations? How do we know that we will be happier being married than staying single? How do we know whether we will be happier in a job that pays less but is nevertheless much closer to home? How can we be sure that rationality will not fail us when we have to face dilemmas that we have never faced before?

So now we've come full circle: economists' description of how the world works – though somewhat incomplete – actually turns out to be useful advice on what we *should* do in situations where we have had little or no prior experience. According to theories on rational choice,[14] there are perhaps two essential ingredients to successful decision-making when a degree of rationality is involved. The first is *time*. Unlike the emotional part of our brain where all decision-making is done instantaneously, the rational part of our brain needs time to think things over, to mull over the information. The second ingredient is getting the *right information*. It's important that we have perfect awareness of all relevant information regarding the outcome of our choice before making a decision, especially one that could change our lives.

Since we can often find time to think things over before coming up with a solution for many of our life problems, could it just be the case that we don't always have the right information about the choices we plan to make? Going back to the unhappy dentist, could it be possible that he decided to obtain a degree in dentistry on a whim or, worse, on a dare? Maybe. Nevertheless, considering the potentially life-changing impact of choosing the right career, it's perhaps more likely that he *did* try to seek all the available information about how happy a career in dentistry would make him in eighteen years' time. How could he then have been so wrong?

There are usually two ways of getting the information we need about the potential impacts of a novel experience. First, we can do some research about the experience. So in the case of the unhappy dentist, his decision to study dentistry could have been influenced by what he was expecting to get objectively from becoming a dentist, such as financial return, or by other people's accounts of their subjective experiences as dentists, or even by conventional wisdom passed down from generation to generation.

Second, if all else fails, we can still use our imagination to conjure up the information we need to undertake a decision. We can try, for example, to picture ourselves in the future: what life would be like being married, or having kids, or having so much money we don't know what to do with it.

The trouble – and we know it's never going to be good news when a sentence starts with 'The trouble' – with these two ways of gathering the necessary information for our rational brain to digest is that both are subject to serious cognitive distortions. Take asking other people about their subjective experiences, for example. Would everybody admit, as the unhappy dentist admits after a few drinks, that they regret undertaking a decision, one that they can't redo or undo? Not always, as it turns out. Studies in psychology suggest that people tend to rationalise the costs of their decisions – especially the ones that can't be undone, such as parenthood or career choices – and then conclude that, given the high price they pay, they must be happy with their choices.[15] In other words, we are more likely to look for and find a positive view of the things we are *stuck with* than of the things we are not.[16]

Our very own imagination is not much better. For example, research in psychology has found that we tend to overestimate the length or the intensity of our feelings – both pleasant and unpleasant – whenever we make a prediction about our future emotional states. Daniel Gilbert and his colleagues illustrated by a series of experiments that people overestimated, by a long shot, the duration of their emotional reactions to various negative events that included, among other things, the break-up of a romantic relationship, rejection from a job interview, and an account of a child's death.[17] The psychologists attributed this so-called 'impact bias' to the fact that, whenever we attempt to predict our affective reactions to a particular event, we naturally focus our attention on that event to the exclusion of others.[18] So, for example, in the case of Gilbert's study, when a mother is asked to imagine what life would be like seven years after the death of her child, she is likely to focus exclusively on the tragedy and fail to consider the many other events that will also happen along the way, and which may also affect her general happiness state. Of course, it would seem absurd for any mother to pause and consider how her unhappiness might be eased by a holiday in the Bahamas, a promotion at work, or seeing a good film over that time period. But the truth is that life does go on, and the things we don't normally think about when imagining our emotional reactions to a particular event do happen and do have affective consequences. It's also the very reason why we often find our future selves not as happy (or unhappy) about a particular event as we thought we would be when we first imagined experiencing it.

So our search for happiness goes on in a somewhat stumbling manner. Sometimes we learn from our past mistakes; sometimes we don't. Sometimes we make the right decision just from asking other people about their affective experiences; sometimes we don't. Sometimes we make a spot-on prediction about the duration and intensity of our affective reactions to a particular event; most of the time we don't. It doesn't matter how hard we try, there just doesn't seem to be a formula to happiness, especially one that is scientifically credible.

Or is there?

The happiness equation

This brings us to the present. What if there *is* a scientific way of constructing a happiness formula? What if we can, with some degree of accuracy, measure and study a *typical* person's emotional reactions to different life events, and then write a complete guidebook about the average impact of each one of them on our well-being? What if there's no need any more for us to ask other people for advice about a particular experience, or use our own imagination to picture what life would be like in the future if we made this choice and not the other? What if we could go back in time to eighteen years ago and say to that unhappy dentist-to-be: 'Hey! Don't become a dentist! You're guaranteed to be miserable for life', even if we're not dentists ourselves? How would we react to that kind of information? What if we can actually put a value or a price on each different life event so that we know which is more worth our time, relative to the others? Will this new knowledge change anything or everything in the way we think or act?

This book is hardly the definitive book about all the things that *really* make each and every one of us happy. That book doesn't exist and probably never will. Rather, this book is about the journey towards achieving that kind of possibility; the possibility of having *perfect foresight* about our emotional reactions to the many different events our lives have to offer. Weaving together findings and theories from the new science of happiness, this book provides a snapshot of what the world would be like if we could truly measure people's happiness and use the data to answer previously 'unanswerable' questions, many of which are absurdly controversial. Does money make us happy? If so, then by *how much* does money make us happy? And if not, then why not? Would we be happier married than remaining single? If so, for how long would we stay happy? How about divorce? Will having children make us happy? What matters in a job? How unhappy will we be after the death of someone we love? And if we want to be compensated for that kind of tragedy, how much money would be enough to make us feel indifferent about the death of our child or partner? How much is a friendship worth? To what extent can my happiness make my partner and my children happier? Will I become more productive, more generous, and live longer if I'm happier today? Would I like any of the answers to these questions? And more importantly, would they change the way I make decisions? Should the government be involved in trying to make me and everyone else happier? I attempt to answer these important questions as best I can by drawing on my own experience in the field of the economics and psychology of happiness, as well as research ideas and findings from the key players in the arena, including, among others, Richard Easterlin, Daniel Kahneman and Andrew Oswald.

Here's my plan of attack.

In Chapter 2, 'Happiness – what has science got to do with it?', I will set the scene for the book by telling you about the history behind the science of happiness; the long feud between economists whose central tenet is 'objectivity' – i.e., what you can't see, you can't measure – and psychologists who believe that human happiness can't be understood without, in part, listening to what people have to say; and how recent improvements in technology and survey designs have helped bridge the gap between these two important fields.

The first and foremost question about our happiness will be tackled in Chapter 3, 'Money can't buy me love, but can it buy me happiness?'. For centuries, we have been wired to believe that an absolute increase in our incomes will automatically make us happier with our lives. But is that always the case? In this chapter, I will tell you about the importance of relative incomes and how this can be used to explain the paradox of happiness, i.e., that the rich are often observed to be happier than the poor, yet an increase in incomes for all doesn't always lead to an increase in happiness for all. I will also tell you how evolution can help explain why, despite the existence of this income–happiness paradox, the pursuit of relative wealth continues to be one of human beings' primal motivations.

There are opportunity costs to almost all of our decisions. In order to be economically efficient, one choice often means that we have to go without another. But how do we know whether a choice is better than the one forgone? How do we make comparisons between life experiences, some of which can't be bought or sold in the marketplace? In Chapters 4 and 5, 'The price of what money can't buy', Parts I and II, I will tell you about the causality issue in happiness studies, what we need to be concerned with when estimating a simple happiness equation, and how we can calculate the true effects of many of our life events, including an absolute increase in our incomes, on our happiness. I will then tell you how we can actually calculate how much money will need to be given to somebody who is either friendless, or single, or is experiencing a bereavement, to be 'just' as happy as if they had an active social life, were married, or had not experienced the death of a loved one.

In Chapters 6 to 8, I will tell you how the price tags of these life events can vary significantly across different environments and over time. I will also tell you how a shift in the allocation of our attention can make one thing easier to cope with, while making another difficult to live with; and also how a misallocation of our attention can make us overestimate the well-being impact of some of the things in our lives – like winning a lottery and having children – when their true effects are actually almost negligible.

So why should we care about the need to try to improve everyone's happiness? In Chapter 9, 'Why should we be happy?', I will tell you about the social benefits of happiness; how happiness can be contagious and how big the contagion could be. I will also tell you about the beneficial impacts of happiness upon our productivity, health, and various pro-social behaviours.

Finally, who should decide what we should do in order to improve our well-being further? Of course, a natural answer to this question is ourselves: we should be in charge of our own happiness. But what if that also fails? Should the government then intervene? In Chapter 10, 'Who gets to decide?', I will tell you about the opposing views: for and against the government's involvement in trying to make the nation happier. Can there be a middle-way solution to this?

This book is also an account of a personal journey, the attempt to satisfy many of my own curiosities about the true determinants of happiness. I hope that it will help you to form your own hypotheses about what really makes us happy, and to question the credibility of our past experiences, our prior beliefs, and our own ability to imagine.

CHAPTER 2

Happiness – what has science got to do with it?

Imagine yourself waking up one sunny morning. It's been rain-ing for days, but this morning the sky is bright blue and there's virtually no cloud in sight. The birds outside your bedroom window are happily chirping away. You've slept a full ten hours, which is something you haven't done for a long time. You turn to your left and see the love of your life lying there peacefully. You smile to yourself and think: 'My life is perfect.'

Rewind.

Imagine yourself waking up one sunny morning. It's been raining for days, but this morning the sky is bright blue and there's virtually no cloud in sight. The birds outside your bed-room windows are happily chirping away. You've slept a full ten hours, which is something you haven't done for a long time. You turn to your left and see $500,000 in crisp banknotes – that's 5,000 Benjamin Franklins staring back at you. You smile to yourself and think: 'My life is perfect.'

There's something not quite right about this picture. To many of us, the thought of swapping the love of our life for a $500,000 pay cheque seems preposterous and disturbing at the same time. Waking up next to the one we love is priceless, I hear you say. No amount of money could ever replace that. And I, for one, couldn't agree more.

But let me play devil's advocate for just a moment. Imagine the following scenario. Sarah has been married to Bob for more than ten years. They share many happy memories together, and have never been apart for more than a week ever since their wedding day. But then tragedy strikes. Bob dies following a fall from the building he's working on.[1] When the news of Bob's death reaches Sarah, it engulfs her and shatters her world into pieces. A couple of weeks after Bob's funeral, Sarah's family lawyer tells her that she should seek compensation for the diminution of quality of life following the death of her husband. In court, the judge agrees that Sarah should be compensated for the non-pecuniary losses associated with Bob's death, and awards her a lump-sum, one-off payment of £10,000 (approximately $15,000 at 2010 prices), which happens to be the compensation package for bereavements normally awarded in tort cases in the UK.[2]

Is a £10,000 payment for her husband's untimely death too small for Sarah when Bob's life was priceless to her? Of course, the court couldn't have awarded a 'priceless' sum of money, as this is unfeasible in any circumstances. But £10,000 compensation for diminished quality of life for the one who remains behind sounds like an insult to any widows and widowers out there. So what should the court do? We can't measure Sarah's loss of happiness following Bob's death and put a price on it now, can we?

Can we?

* * *

'Let's study death!'

I couldn't believe my ears when I first heard this said to me over a plate of sashimi and hot green tea. But as I let the words sink in, I remembered one of the things I have learned over the years from working with Andrew Oswald, a professor of economics at the University of Warwick and one of the world's most respected experts on the economics of happiness – which is always to expect the unexpected. It was the end of summer in 2005, and it had been a while since Andrew and I had last got together; in fact, we hadn't seen each other since I took up my first post as a research officer at the Institute of Education, University of London. And so it wasn't until Andrew emailed me one afternoon to say that he was coming down to London for a day that we decided to meet up at one of those tacky Japanese restaurants off Goodge Street tube station.

'Eric Posner and Cass Sunstein at the University of Chicago are organising a conference on legal implications of the new research on happiness, and they want us to write something for it. So let's do something on death and happiness,' he beamed.

Bentham, Robbins and Hicks

The idea that we can study the interplay between death and happiness seems far-fetched, but certainly not impossible – at least, not any more. For over 200 years since the British economist and philosopher Jeremy Bentham's first creation of the 'felicific calculus' – an algorithm used to calculate the degree or amount of pleasure that a specific action is likely to cause[3] – the notion that happiness should be measured and studied has taken quite a battering from people in academia. Leading the charge against Bentham's so-called 'happiness calculator' in the early 1930s were Lionel Robbins and John Hicks, two of the most prominent economists of the time.

The method of simply asking people to report their levels of happiness is unscientific, chorused the two dons. Since happiness is subjective, we can't compare one person's happiness with another person's happiness. Unlike money, the happiness of two different people is considered incommensurable. We can't add it or subtract it. We can't count it or put it in a jar for future use. We can't even see it. The lack of *interpersonal comparability* makes happiness something of a defunct concept. If we can't really compare happiness, then why should we bother measuring it?

Both Robbins and Hicks went on to argue that we can work out what is good for the people in a given society by simply observing their behaviours or 'revealed preferences'. If person A chooses to eat an orange rather than an apple, assuming that A is rational (in that A always makes careful, logical calculations before making any decisions), then it's reasonable to say that A prefers oranges to apples and that eating oranges makes A happier than eating apples. We don't even need to know *how much* in metric terms an orange can make A happier than an apple can. All we really need to know in order to work out what makes people happy is the ordinal ranking of these preferences.[4] Ergo, according to both Robbins and Hicks, happiness as we knew it is dead. Rest in peace, Jeremy Bentham; it seems that we, the neoclassical economists, have the final word.

The psychologists' fortress

But out in the wilderness, away from the critical and judgemental eyes of economists, were hundreds of psychologists working on the same idea as Bentham: that happiness is quantifiable and should therefore be measured. As an attitude that is not accessible to public observation, these psychologists believed that a concept such as happiness should be studied, in part, by asking how people feel. They embarked on their research journey by asking hundreds and thousands of individuals some of the following examples of happiness questions:

'Taken all things together, how happy would you say you are these days? Would you say you are very happy, pretty happy, or not too happy?'

'On the whole are you very satisfied, fairly satisfied, not very satisfied, or not satisfied with the life that you lead?'

'Have you recently been feeling reasonably happy, all things considered? More so than usual, same as usual, less so than usual, or much less than usual?'

Each response to these happiness (or life satisfaction)[5] questions was then given a numerical score; so, for example, the response to the first happiness question is coded so that 'Not too happy' is given a value of 1, 'Pretty happy' a value of 2, and 'Very happy' a value of 3.[6] And for decades, psychologists have been showing that these 'happiness data' are not what economists believed them to be – i.e. just random noises – by showing that they in fact correlate really well with participants' subjective recalls of positive and negative events that took place in their life,[7] assessments of how happy they are by their friends and family,[8] and reports from clinical experts,[9] as well as the duration of the genuine or so-called 'Duchenne' smile,[10] and measures of response to stress such as heart rate and blood pressure.[11] Not to mention that these responses to the happiness questions have been shown by psychologists to predict, with reasonable accuracy, the risk of getting coronary heart disease in the future.[12]

The rapid technological advances in medical research over the past several decades have allowed Richard Davidson, a professor of psychology and psychiatry at the University of Wisconsin, to take the debate on whether or not happiness is measurable to a new level. In his seminal study published in 2000, Davidson and his research team asked a group of randomly selected volunteers to enter a functional magnetic resonance imaging (fMRI) machine in order for their brains to be scanned. While lying face-up in the machine, the volunteers were shown two different photographs: one of a happy, smiling baby and the other of a baby with clear physical deformity. The fMRI machine, which is normally used to record the flow of oxygen to replace the energy used up in electrical activity, showed some striking images of brain activity while the volunteers were shown these two photographs.

When the volunteers were asked to closely examine the photograph of a smiling baby, the fMRI scan picked up a significant flow of oxygen to the left side of their prefrontal cortex (the anterior part of the frontal lobes of the brain). By contrast, when the photo of a severely deformed baby was shown to them, it was the right side of their prefrontal cortex that was activated.[13] Davidson's main conclusion was that positive feelings correspond to the left side of the brain, while negative feelings correspond to the right side of the brain.

Davidson followed this up with another powerful study, but this time an electroencephalography (EEG) analysis was used on volunteers instead of the fMRI machine. The aim was to study how people who have been experiencing different emotions react when they are prompted to evaluate their own feelings. By using EEG to record the electrical activity along the scalp generated by the firing of neurons within the brain, Davidson and his team were able to show that people whose left side of the brain was especially active ('left-siders') were likely to report more positive feelings than those whose right side of the brain was more active ('right-siders'). They also smiled more and were assessed to be happy by their friends and family. By contrast, the right-siders reported more negative feelings, smiled less, and were rated as unhappy by their friends and family.[14]

In the late 1980s, in an equally groundbreaking study, the American professor of neurology and epidemiology David Snowdon began his pet project on ageing and Alzheimer's disease by conducting a longitudinal study – a study that tracks the same individuals over long periods of time – of a group of American Catholic women who became members of the Sisters School of Notre Dame in 1932. The sisters, on joining the order, were each asked to write an autobiography. And it's these hand-written autobiographies that were the subject of Snowdon's interest.

For hours on end, Snowdon and his research team counted the number of times each nun used positive words and negative words in her autobiography. So, for a lucid example, the following extracts demonstrate the differences between what Snowdon classified respectively (and informally) as the 'happy' and the 'not-so-happy' nuns:

Sister 1 (low positive emotion): I was born on September 26, 1909, the eldest of seven children, five girls and two boys ... My candidate year was spent in the Motherhouse, teaching Chemistry and Second Year Latin at Notre Dame Institute. With God's grace, I intend to do my best for our Order, for the spread of religion and for my personal sanctification.

Sister 2 (high positive emotion): God started my life off well by bestowing upon me a grace of inestimable value ... The past year which I have spent as a candidate study-ing at Notre Dame College has been a very happy one. Now I look forward with eager joy to receiving the Holy Habit of Our Lady and to a life of union with Love Divine.

Once in the nunnery, the sisters followed the same diet and the same daily rituals, which included morning and evening prayers, as well as charitable works and the day-to-day chores.

Their 'same food, same work, same routine' ritual provided Snowdon with a very powerful tool to study the ageing process of these nuns, as it helped him to minimise unexpected extraneous variables that may have confounded other research. What he and his team found was something remarkable.

Among the group of 'not-so-happy' nuns, only 40 per cent lived to see their 85th birthday. Among the 'happy' nuns, almost 90 per cent lived to pass their 85th milestone. On average, concluded Snowdon, the group containing the most positive nuns lived nine years longer than the group containing the least positive nuns.[15] This is a huge effect when you think that smoking takes approximately three years off your life.[16]

Happy people live longer, so to speak.

And more recently, four psychologists from the UK, together with a dermatologist and a physiotherapist in the US, decided to take the 'happiness is good for your health' research to another level. In a study published in *Psychoneuroendocrinology* (yes, that really *is* the name of the journal) in 2004, Marcel Ebrecht, Justin Hextall, Lauren-Grace Kirtley, Alice Taylor, Mary Dyson and John Weinman presented evidence that people's self-reported level of stress correlates nicely with how quickly the same people heal from a puncture wound.

It may sound a bit cruel, but their experiment involved giving each of their 24 male non-smoker participants a standard 4mm-punch biopsy (a procedure involving the removal of cells or tissues for examination). They then had their healing progress monitored via high-resolution ultrasound scanning. The participants were also asked, as part of the experiment, to report how stressed they were two weeks before, directly after, and two weeks after the biopsy. What they found was astounding: people who reported being more stressed at the time of the biopsy healed significantly more slowly than those who were reportedly less stressed by having a 4mm needle punching the skin. In other words, happy people may not only live longer than less happy people, they may also heal more quickly from physical wounds.

And so here we have, perhaps for the first time, strong objective evidence to support the idea that happiness is indeed measurable. It can also be used to predict something useful, and is therefore worth further scientific investigation. Viva Bentham!

* * *

Earlier, in the late 1940s, radical ideas had begun to emerge from a small group of economists that maybe – just maybe – human beings are not as rational as we think we are. One of the most provocative ideas at the time was the one proposed by the American economist James Duesenberry. According to Duesenberry, our behaviours are shaped not only by a set of abstract rules that we have in our heads but also by the behaviours of other people in the community.

According to the mainstream economic theory on consumption, the 'permanent-income hypothesis', a family's current spending depends not on its current income, but rather on its long-run average (or permanent) income. First proposed by the Nobel laureate Milton Friedman, the permanent-income hypothesis predicts that people – assuming that they are perfectly rational – prefer steady-state consumption paths to highly volatile ones, and that transitory or short-term changes in income have little or no effect on how people choose to consume or spend their money.[17] What this implies is that consumption depends absolutely on what people expect to earn over their lifetime, and not on how other people spend their incomes. A recent MIT business graduate trainee in an investment firm should, in principle, have a higher level of consumption than a Ph.D. graduate in history from York, even if both are currently earning the same income. The business graduate looks ahead to a much higher future income, and thus consumes accordingly, all because she knows she can afford to.

Duesenberry, on the other hand, argued that an individual's decision to consume depends more on the desire to emulate one's neighbours and less on one's own abstract standard of living.[18] According to what was later called Duesenberry's 'relative-income hypothesis', the Ph.D. graduate in history will start spending *more* of his current income if he sees that his neighbour, the MIT business graduate, spends more, regardless of whether or not they will go on to earn different incomes over their lifetimes.

The idea that people will go out of their way to spend more of their current income in order to 'keep up with the Joneses' was, at the time, very hard to swallow for mainstream economists. To many, the idea that our preferences are significantly determined by behaviours of other people seemed both erratic and irrational. I bought a Honda because I like and can afford a Honda – not because my neighbour owns a Honda and I would be very unhappy if I didn't own one!

So who's right then? Is it Milton Friedman – a guy who won the Nobel Prize in Economics for his theory on consumption behaviour? Or is it James Duesenberry – a long-forgotten economist whose name is virtually unknown unless you're near retirement?

It was Duesenberry, of course, hands down.

According to economist Robert Frank, Friedman's permanent-income hypothesis has always been outperformed empirically by Duesenberry's relative-income hypothesis, ever since their conceptions at approximately the same time in the 1950s.[19]

For one thing, the permanent-income hypothesis is unable to explain satisfactorily why, as everyone in a nation becomes richer, the national savings rates (i.e. the average savings rates of everyone in the economy) do not rise in parallel – when, at any given point in time, the rich are normally observed to save at higher rates than the poor. Given the importance of these two contradictory patterns in the data, Friedman simply dismissed the high savings rates among the rich as a statistical artefact. A blip in the data set. He essentially argued that, if we were to take into account the influences of life-cycle differences and transitory earnings of everybody in an economy, we should see high-income persons saving the same fractions of their incomes as low-income persons. And yet no study has been able to provide any evidence to support Friedman's claim.

By contrast, such a paradox fits more with Duesenberry's argument that poverty is in fact relative. The poor save at lower rates simply because they feel that they should try to catch up with the higher spending of others. In other words, their aspirations are assumed to rise in proportion to the rise in their income. Assuming that the poor's need to catch up with the rich will persist no matter how much national income grows, it's no wonder that national savings rates have failed to rise with national income in the US over time. Put simply, Duesenberry's relative-income hypothesis seems to describe better than Friedman's permanent-income hypothesis how human beings actually behave in real life.

And so it appears that our decisions – whether to save, to spend, perhaps even to fall in love with someone – may be influenced more by the context in which we are living and less by our own absolute standard of living. What does this information mean to social scientists? Does it mean that we can't rely on the traditional method of merely observing individuals' behaviours in order to work out what's good for them? Does it mean that people may not always choose to do or consume the things that maximise their happiness? Does it mean that there's a possibility, even if it's a tiny one, that traditional economic textbooks may have made the wrong decision in dismissing altogether from their analyses Bentham's idea that happiness should be measured, quantified and studied?

Yes, yes, and absolutely yes.

The birth of statistical wizards

The apparent divide between two social-science disciplines is scientifically unattractive. But trying to convince hard-nosed economists to believe beyond their reasonable doubt that the self-reported happiness data sets frequently used by psychologists are valid – that they truly measure something useful – is like trying to paint a town red using a very small toothbrush. As we've seen, the main argument of economists against the use of such 'frivolous' measures of someone's well-being in economic analysis is that, theoretically, happiness is not an interpersonally comparable variable. (On the reported happiness scale, for example, your '1' may be my '3', or your 'Very satisfied with life' may be my 'Yeah, so-so'.) The internal happiness scale between young and old, male and female, and rich and poor may be very different. And so, for traditional economists, it doesn't matter whether these happiness data have been shown to predict coronary heart disease or life expectancy (they could just be correlations born out of pure coincidence). If it's theoretically undeniable that the way I normally rate my happiness is systematically different to how other people would normally rate their happiness, then this fact alone is enough for economists to give happiness data sets the cold shoulder.

Yet Yew-Kwang Ng, a philosophical and theoretical welfare economist, argued that the majority of traditional economists may have been too 'heavily brainwashed' with the idea that cardinal measures of utility (or happiness) are meaningless (see below for a definition of cardinal).[20] Each of us – he proposed in an article published in 1997 in the prestigious *Economic Journal* – wants money, not for its own sake, but for what it can bring us in terms of happiness.[21] And for this reason, if bundle A (or whatever it may be) makes me twice as happy as bundle B, then it's perfectly sensible to say that I prefer bundle A *twice as much* as bundle B. Happiness, in this case, can therefore be written directly into our preference function – which is, after all, an interpersonally comparable and a quantifiable concept.

While advances in economic theory alone – thanks to the pioneering work by Ng – may have been enough to convince any disbelieving theorists that happiness is comparable across individuals in a population, the same can hardly be said for econometricians (or the other half of the world's economists), whose expertise is in the application of good, statistical methods in the study of economic principles. According to them, self-reported happiness scores are not *cardinally* measured (i.e., a change in the happiness score from a 1 to a 2 for one individual isn't necessarily the same as a change in the happiness score from a 2 to a 3 for other individuals). They are, by their very nature, *ordinal* variables. What this means is that we can claim only that someone's happiness score of a 3 is preferred to his or her own abstract internal score of a 2, and that his or her score of a 2 is preferred to a 1. However, the distance between these numbers is *a priori* unknown.

Of course, what these econometricians are ultimately implying is that any kind of estimation that assumes happiness to be a cardinally measured variable is, statistically-speaking, meaningless.

But unbeknown to many of these critical econometricians when they first expressed their reservations about the validity of these happiness data, in 1975 two statistical and mathematical geniuses, Richard McKelvey and William Zavoina, had already published an article in the *Journal of Mathematical Sociology* outlining a statistical method that can be used to analyse variables that are measured in order.[22] Their idea is simple and straightforward. For one thing, there's no need to assume cardinality in the reported happiness numbers (i.e. that the difference in happiness between a 3 and a 2 for any individual is the same as between a 2 and a 1 for any other individual). The only assumption we need to make about the property of happiness data is that a reported happiness score of 3 corresponds to a higher level of happiness than a reported happiness score of 2, and so on in that order for all individuals.

This ordinal comparability assumption implies that individuals share a common opinion of what happiness is. It relies on supporting evidence from two psychological findings. The first is that individuals are generally able to recognise and predict the satisfaction levels of others: in interviews in which respondents are shown pictures or videos of other individuals, they are reasonably accurate in identifying whether the individual is happy, jealous, angry, etc.[23] And the second is that individuals in the same language community have a common understanding of how to translate inner feelings into a number scale, simply in order for individuals to be able to communicate with each other.[24]

By applying McKelvey and Zavoina's so-called 'ordered probit' model on self-reported happiness data, researchers can find out, for example, what is the average probability of a married person being 'very happy with life' compared to someone who is single, all else being equal. This – perhaps unexpectedly – proved to be a major methodological breakthrough for a minority of economists who, like psychologists, were interested in subjective well-being data but whose work was, back then, widely discredited by their peers.[25] And with the help of further research and refinements of McKelvey and Zavoina's model – subsequent researchers found that assuming ordinality or cardinality on happiness scores makes virtually no difference to the interpretation of happiness estimates and that we can add, subtract, or average happiness scores of people within the same country as we please[26] – there was no looking back for these daredevil 'happiness' economists. And soon enough, the study of the causes and correlates of human happiness became one of the hottest topics in economics, with both the size and depth of literature increasing at an exponential rate over the last decade.[27]

A badly burnt bridge between the two social-science disciplines had – thanks to the two statistical wizards – been rebuilt stronger than ever before.

* * *

So what do you think?'

I appeared to have forgotten to give Andrew an answer. An analysis on death and happiness seemed a tricky thing to do. We would probably get hammered by the press as well. I could picture it now, a headline in the *Daily Mail*: 'Two Experts Put a Price Tag on Death! Have They No Sympathy for the Dead?'

I decided to throw caution to the winds. 'What the heck,' I said. 'Let's do it!'

CHAPTER 3

MONEY CAN'T BUY ME LOVE, BUT CAN IT BUY ME HAPPINESS?

If somebody asked you, 'Would you be happier if you were richer?', what do you think your response would be? 'Yes, of course!' would be my guess. Perhaps unsurprisingly, it's not so hard to understand why the word 'money' is often used synonymously with the word 'happiness'. Not only does money provide us with the basic foundation for survival, but at least in the marketable world it also allows us the chance to obtain whatever we want that is normally purchasable in the market. The existing view that there is this one-to-one relationship between money and happiness is further bolstered by conventional wisdom about the value of money: most of us have been brought up in a world where the importance of money has been thrust upon us with mind-numbing ferocity by our parents, our friends, our neighbours, even the men and women on our television sets.

In other words, we have been brought up in a world where the pursuit of happiness is virtually the pursuit of personal wealth. And that seems to be the same principle used everywhere in the world.[1] We were told that more is always better, and most of us grew up thinking that there's no need to question what seems like an open-and-shut case.

Well, not if Richard Easterlin has anything to say about it.

The professor and his paradox
Born in 1926 in Ridgefield Park, New Jersey, Richard Easterlin knew from the very beginning of his academic career that he wasn't going to be one of those run-of-the-mill

I-can-tell-why-you-are-standing-in-the-unemployment-line economists. After receiving his Ph.D. in economics from the University of Pennsylvania in 1953, Easterlin embarked on what was to be a very long career conducting research on demography. At a time when the fashion among economists was to sit in the office and draw up theoretical models to explain how the world works, Easterlin preferred to busy himself with countless numbers of data sets and spent hours on end working with thousands – sometimes millions – of observations of real-world situations. He was keen to find empirical evidence to answer such oddball questions as: How can people's fertility behaviour be explained using economic principles? What are the impacts of rising material aspirations on already scarce world resources? And what are the implications of the American baby boom on the subsequent number of elderly widows living alone?

But it wasn't until the early 1970s that he made one of the biggest contributions to our understanding of the relationship between money and happiness. Famously rejected by the influential *American Economic Review* before eventually finding its home in 1974 as a chapter in a book on economic growth,[2] Richard Easterlin's influential paper on the relationship between economic growth and happiness ended up shaking the very foundations of established economic theory. His hypotheses were simple. Are the wealthy members of society usually happier than the poor? And are we getting happier as our country becomes richer over time?

Using self-reported happiness data collected during the post-war period,[3] Easterlin found that less than a quarter of the poorest Americans (with an income of less than $3,000 per annum) reported that they were 'very happy'. On the other hand, nearly half of the richest Americans (income of $15,000 or more per annum) reported to be 'very happy'; that's twice as many as in the poorest group. A similar pattern was repeated for other countries in Asia, Africa and Latin America. In other words, rich people were found to be a lot happier than poor people, regardless of where they were in the world.

That, of course, doesn't seem very surprising. It is, after all, consistent with what we already believe to be true – that money makes people happy.

Well, if that's the case, then we should expect to see the same pattern emerging in the relationship between income and happiness over time. Provided that richer people are happier people, then undoubtedly an increase in income for *everyone* in the country should also lead to a happier society as a whole, right? A richer self is much better than a poorer self, correct?

Far from it.

Although there is strong within-country evidence that richer people are significantly happier than poorer people, Easterlin presented counter-evidence that an increase in income for all does not lead to an increase in happiness for all. Take America, for example. The United States experienced continued economic growth for 50 years after the end of the Second World War. This is clear from looking at the average real income or gross domestic product (GDP) per capita, which rose annually for most Americans for the latter part of the 20th century.

The trouble is, aggregate happiness didn't really rise with it at all (see Figure 1).

Richard Easterlin's evidence that an increase in income of all does not increase the happiness of all – even though the rich are significantly happier than the poor – is understandably a bitter pill to swallow for many who believe that the pursuit of greater wealth is everyone's sure way to a happier life. And so far he seems to be right, as well; since its first publication in 1974, there have been many subsequent studies, most prominently by

Year	Average happiness levels	Real GDP per capita
1975	2.20	$22,592
1980	2.20	$25,640
1985	2.22	$28,781
1990	2.23	$32,112
1995	2.20	$34,111

Figure 1. An illustration of the Easterlin Paradox: an increase in income does not lead to an increase in aggregate happiness levels. The mean happiness is on a 3-point happiness scale, where 1 = 'Not so happy', 2 = 'Pretty happy', 3 = 'Very happy'.
Source: General Social Survey, USA.

Easterlin himself, to suggest that the 'paradox' isn't just a US phenomenon. The same picture can also be drawn for Japan[4] and many of the Western European countries, including the UK, France, Germany and Italy.[5] And despite a few articles claiming that there is indeed a positive relationship between economic growth and happiness,[6] the overall evidence is still very much on the side of what Richard Easterlin originally found.[7]

The really important question, then, is: What explains why richer people are happier than poorer people but more money doesn't seem to make society as a whole any happier?

It's all relative

'Men do not desire to be rich, but richer than other men.'
John Stuart Mill

Have you ever been to a football match where all the other spectators were of the same height as you? Me neither; usually everyone else is a lot taller than me.[8] But let's imagine for a change that everybody shares roughly the same height. Imagine also that you have bought yourself a seat right in the middle of the stadium. The view is good: you can see the full length of the pitch and all the players on it without having to crane your neck too much.

But then, about twenty minutes into the game, all the people who have been sitting in front of you decide to stand up in unison, perhaps trying to get a closer look at some incident on the pitch. You suddenly find yourself completely obscured from the football match you paid good money for. Assuming that you – and everybody else in the stadium – are the type that tends to follow rather than defy the norm, your knee-jerk reaction is probably to stand up with the rest of the crowd. This means that those sitting right behind you have to stand up too. Within minutes, everybody in the stadium is watching the match standing up from their comfortable seats. And even though standing up is making your legs ache, you can't really sit down for long while the people in front of you still refuse to sit down.[9]

There's a very simple point to this story: given that everybody's height is approximately the same, there will be no real difference in the viewing outcomes whether everyone is watching the match standing up or sitting down. Only that the former is perhaps a little more tiring than the latter.

But how does that relate to the paradoxical relationship between money and happiness?

* * *

What traditional economics textbooks don't tell you is that there are two main motivations for the demand for money. The first is for pure consumption: we demand money for its unique function as a medium of exchange for all the goods and services

34

we need to survive adequately. The second – and lesser known one – is that we demand money for the *status* that it brings.

For poor people, the effect of income upon general well-being can be more physical than psychological; having more money means, for example, that we can now drive to work and not have to walk endless miles every day. But a change from owning an affordable Austin Maestro to owning a luxurious Aston Martin in an era of excess will not make a lot of difference to our overall standard of living.[10] After all, both cars should still be able to get us from point A to point B (provided that we drive carefully). One might get us there a little faster than the other, of course, but the price difference between the two cars (a new Aston Martin is likely to be at least £85,000 more expensive than a used Maestro) might seem to many to be hardly worth it.

But people don't buy an Aston Martin for the mere fact that it can get them to the end of the road faster than a Maestro can. People buy an Aston Martin largely because it can get them to the end of the road with the kind of panache money can buy. Put simply, once we go beyond a certain level of income, it becomes natural for most of us to start caring a lot more about what other people think of us, about whether other people know how much money we have deposited in our bank account compared to their bank account.

It may sound a little irrational, and perhaps I'm slightly exaggerating the point I'm trying to make. But there really is a great deal of evidence to suggest that our happiness is not only a function of our own income but also of other people's incomes. Take our happiness at the workplace, for example. British economists Andrew Oswald and Andrew Clark are among the pioneers investigating and estimating the effect of 'the average incomes of people like me' – in this particular case, referring to those in both full-time and part-time employment, aged sixteen and over – on how happy we are at work.[11] Using a nationally representative sample of the British workforce in 1991, the two Andrews show that there is indeed a negative effect of other people's incomes on our self-reported job satisfaction. Moreover, they also find the well-being effect of our own income and other people's incomes to be *equal* and *opposite*. In other words, receiving a pay rise at work will certainly make me a happier worker. But if other people are getting exactly the same pay rise as I do – well, all of us might as well receive no rise at all.[12]

But it's not just the way we evaluate how happy we are at work that is subject to the effect of other people's earnings. Spanish economist Ada Ferrer-i-Carbonell of the Institute of Economic Analysis in Barcelona is able to show that the incomes of other people who are of the same sex, age and education as me can also affect *negatively* the way I rate how my life is going as a whole.[13] Representing only a handful of female economists working on happiness, Ada demonstrates that the larger people's income is in comparison to those who share the same socio-demographic characteristics, the more satisfied with life they will be. Like Andrew Oswald and Andrew Clark before her, she concludes that increases in family income accompanied by identical increases in the income of other 'people like me' increases the happiness of no one.

One question of interest is: Who exactly do we compare ourselves with? Is it just people of the same sex, age and education as us? Or could it be our friends, our work colleagues, our neighbours, our romantic partners, our brothers and sisters, our parents? How about ourselves in the past? American economist Erzo Luttmer of Harvard University puts one of these ideas to the test and examines the effect of having a richer neighbour upon our happiness. In an article published in the *Quarterly*

Journal of Economics, Luttmer shows how the average earnings of those who live locally to us really – and I mean *really* – affect one's definition of happiness in America.[14] By carefully teasing out anything that might affect our decision to live in a certain neighbourhood and not another (richer neighbourhoods might have less crime, better local schools and other amenities that raise our happiness) so that he can get as close as possible to estimating the purest, most causal impact of other people's incomes on our happiness, Luttmer is able to demonstrate that an increase in our neighbour's earnings has roughly the same negative effect as a similarly sized decrease in our own income. Interestingly, he also finds that people living in a rich neighbourhood have more frequent open arguments about money with spouses than those living in a poor neighbourhood.

The evidence of a negative relative income effect is not limited only to individuals living in advanced industrialised economies such as the US and the UK. In a unique study of the interplay between happiness and relative incomes, John Knight of Oxford University, together with Lina Song of the University of Nottingham and Ramini Gunatilaka of Monash University, chose instead to explore the effect of other people's incomes upon the happiness of those living in rural China,[15] an economy far removed from the Europe–North America nexus that has until now dominated the literature. By asking the survey respondents directly, 'Who do you compare yourself with?', Knight and his co-authors have done what other studies had not been able to do previously: get to know exactly who the respondents refer to as their reference groups, rather than simply impose one and hope for the best. From their study, it appears that people care a lot more about the incomes of those who live in close proximity to them. The authors find that nearly 70 per cent of the rural Chinese say that they compare themselves with those living in the same village, and only 11 per cent say that their comparison group comes from people outside their village. Holding own income and village income constant, the three economists find respondents who say that their income is much above the village average to be a whole lot happier than those who say their income is much lower than the village average.

But maybe not all comparisons are bad. In some cases, especially among the few studies that focus their attention on finding the determinants of happiness for people living in transitional countries such as post-apartheid South Africa, the Latin American nations and Russia, the psychological impact from living in close proximity with other people who are, on average, richer than oneself is unexpectedly positive.[16] Such an apparent divergence between two conclusions about the effect of relative income on happiness is scientifically unappealing. What is it, then, that makes these individuals in the so-called 'new market economies' different from those in the US, the UK, or even in rural China?

In his influential paper published in the *Quarterly Journal of Economics* in 1973, Albert Hirschman, a renowned political economist and emeritus professor at the Institute of Advanced Study at Princeton University, offered some thoughts on why there may be such a divide in the psychological effect of relative income.[17] Hirschman doesn't argue against the notion that people care deeply about how much they earn compared to how much other people earn. Instead, he argues that the direction of the relative income effect upon our happiness (*negative* versus *positive*) will depend on how it affects our expected future contentment with our income. In other words, in certain circumstances – particularly early on in countries' development paths – individual A may feel a lot better about how his life is turning out after seeing the advancements of individual B, as these gains supply positive information about what the future might be like for A. These positive feelings on expectations may outweigh the feelings of envy that A has for B. Yet if, over time, A does not achieve what B achieves in terms of financial rewards, then these feelings can result in frustration; this is analogous to the negative relative income effect found more often in the literature. Hirschman likens this to being stuck in a traffic jam in a tunnel, where initially those in a stalled lane gain hope from movements in other lanes. But if their lane never moves, then hope may turn to frustration and, in turn, reduce their overall happiness.

So, to recap, the evidence seems to suggest that human beings care a great deal about relative income, about how much other people are earning relative to how much they themselves are earning. Most of the time, depending on where we live in the world, the effect of relative income on our well-being is negative. In other words, money indeed buys happiness, but the higher our relevant others' incomes are, the less happy we seem to be with our own absolute income. Yet it's not just the quantity of other people's money that we care about. Oh no. Relative income is only a small piece of the jigsaw, a proxy for something else that we care even more about. Human beings, it seems, care more about their *rank-ordered position* within a subset of people with whom they associate themselves.[18]

It's clear from casual observation that human beings are deeply interested in rankings: over sports outcomes (Roger Federer retains his number 1 spot again); over exam results (who came first in the English exam?); over university choice (which universities rank in the top five in the league table?); or, more related to the point here, over incomes (who tops the *Forbes* rich list this year?). While the notion of relative income refers to *how much* we have compared to the average (the psychological impact from living in a neighbourhood where the average income is £50 higher than what I normally earn may be different to the psychological impact from living in a neighbourhood where the average income is £20,000 higher than what I normally earn), the notion of income rank is all about relative positions: I don't really care about how much more I earn relative to everyone else in my office or in my neighbourhood – whether it's £50 or £20,000, it doesn't matter – just as long as I'm the richest person among the people I know. That will do me.

The idea seems plausible. But can it really be the case that human beings care a great deal more about where they rank within a subset of people with whom they compare themselves than they care about the average earnings of other people? The British psychologist Gordon Brown and his colleagues at the University of Warwick seem to think so.[19] By examining how the ranking of pay among workers within the same organisation determines how happy they are at work, Brown and co. conclude that while relative income matters significantly to how workers rate their job satisfaction, its impact is eclipsed by that of the effect of relative position, i.e. where they rank in terms of pay within the organisation. It doesn't really matter how much I earn relative to other people, as long as I rank higher than most other people in the organisation.[20]

Human beings, in other words, value their ordinal position per se – and perhaps even above what absolute income can buy in terms of happiness. This provides one of the key explanations for the Easterlin Paradox: why the rich are happier than the poor, but an increase in incomes for all may not increase happiness for all.

But how so?

The two miners' dilemma

Imagine two coal miners, Gary and Robbie, who come for a job interview at the mining company Dig That, Inc. Once they have both been offered a job, they are told that they can choose to work in a clean mine or in a dusty mine. The going rate for working in the clean mine is $200 per week; however, in the dusty mine the going rate is higher at $250 per week. Nevertheless, working in the dusty mine also has its cost: a year's worth of inhaled dust and fumes will most likely result in a shortening of life expectancy for the miner by five years.

If neither Gary nor Robbie cares a great deal about the ordinal position of his income rank within the company, and knowing how damaging the dusty mine would be to their health, each would find it worthwhile to sacrifice $50 to escape working in the dusty mine. Both will earn the same salary, $200 per week, which is plenty to survive on.

But if both Gary and Robbie are strongly concerned about where they rank in the income hierarchy relative to the other person, then the happiness payoff to each will depend in a clear way on the mine chosen by the other. If both care deeply about where they rank in terms of pay, then there is an additional incentive for each to choose the dusty mine over the clean mine. This is simply because neither is willing to sacrifice $50 a week for longevity if in the process he loses ground in the income rank within the organisation. The dominant strategy – or the best strategy regardless of what the other person chooses to do – for both miners is to choose the dusty mine (assuming that each has no control whatsoever over the other's choice). Yet, by doing so, an outcome results that both Gary and Robbie find distasteful in comparison with the feasible alternative of working in the clean mine.

	Robbie: Clean mine	Robbie: Dusty mine
Gary: Clean mine	2nd best option for Gary 2nd best option for Robbie	Worst option for Gary Best option for Robbie
Gary: Dusty mine	Best option for Gary Worst option for Robbie	3rd best option for Gary 3rd best option for Robbie

Figure 2. Clean mine: $200 a week. Dusty mine: $250 a week, but also a reduced life expectancy of five years.

This example of safety choices when relative income matters belongs to Robert Frank, a professor of economics with an illustrious career at Cornell University.[21] His idea is a simple one. If individuals care deeply about income rank, then it's easy to see why they might find it attractive to sacrifice longevity in return for an opportunity to move up the income hierarchy, to be above everyone else in the pecking order. Yet the number of favoured positions in any rank ordering is limited by simple arithmetic. And so the exchange that is so attractive from each individual's point of view has no similar allure when viewed from the perspective of the population as a whole – just as each individual's decision to stand up in the football stadium affects other people's viewing pleasure, which in turn affects their choices.

And what's special about Frank's idea is that it can be used to explain the Easterlin Paradox in a simple yet elegant way. The reason why the rich are happier than the poor within a country at a point in time is not very difficult to understand: rich people have a significantly higher standard of living than poor people. Provided that people also care deeply about relative standing, then there is additional happiness to be gained for the rich from standing tall above everyone else in their comparison group, while the poor will inevitably feel the gloom from being relatively deprived of what others have. However, since the pursuit of relative standing is a 'zero-sum' game (whenever there's a winner, there's also a loser), over time in a given country the effect of an increase in income on aggregate happiness will be via what money can buy in terms of consumption only.[22] This explains why, in certain advanced industrialised economies where the standard of living of the population is already high by absolute standards, an increase in incomes for all does not automatically lead to an increase in happiness for all.

And now that we are here, an important question suggests itself. What's so special about status that it makes us drive ourselves very hard to have it, and sometimes willing to sacrifice longevity to secure it, even when its value depends entirely on something that we really have no control over: other people's status?

In other words, why do human beings care about relative standing per se?

There's something about George W. Bush, Jimmy Carter and Richard Nixon

What did US presidents George W. Bush, Jimmy Carter and Richard Nixon have that other presidents since the 1930s didn't? It must have been something special, because they were the only three presidents since Calvin Coolidge (5'10"), who beat John W. Davis (5'11") in 1924, to take on a taller candidate in presidential elections and win!

There's strong empirical evidence to suggest that height plays an important part in almost every US presidential election: in the past fifteen elections, the taller candidate has won eleven

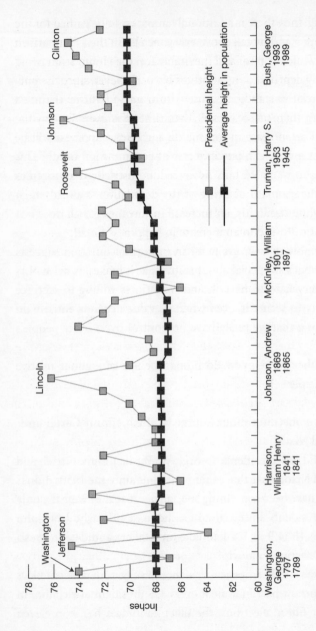

Figure 3. Height of US Presidents

Source: Persico, Postlewaite and Silverman, 'The effect of adolescent experience and labour market outcomes: the case of height', *Journal of Political Economy* (2004).

times (the most recent exception being George W. Bush), and almost every US president since George Washington has tended to be distinctly taller than the general average population.[23]

The beneficial effect of height on personal and professional success not only favours those who want to become the most powerful man in the world. Rather, studies have shown that taller men tend to perform significantly better in the marriage market[24] – which is also one reason why, in the US and the UK, black men, who have historically held lower status compared to white men but at the same time are normally extremely tall by relative standards, are substantially more likely to have white (historically higher-status) spouses than black women, and why Chinese men, who again have historically held lower status than white men and are typically shorter than white men, are half as likely to marry a white person as Chinese women.[25] It's also the reason why taller men have higher average earnings and hold more highly skilled jobs than shorter men.[26]

What is it about height, then, that makes almost anyone who has plenty of it more likely to be successful in life than others? According to theories in social psychology, it's plausible that short people are stigmatised by others at an early age, thus placing them at a disadvantage in negotiating personal dealings.[27] This psychological explanation can be linked directly to theories in evolutionary selection suggesting that there may exist a 'taste' for taller men in our potential employers and mates: as the human species evolved, to the extent that size provided a direct advantage in the competition for resources, a preference for associating with tall people may have been shaped long ago by the process of natural selection. Height, in other words, may have been used as a proxy or 'signal' for good genes, excellent health and lack of deprivation throughout the development process – some of the human attributes that are highly desirable by whoever wants to employ us or marry us. Adding to this, a recent study by two economics professors, Anne Case and Christina Paxson of Princeton University, reveals that height can also be used as a reasonable biomarker of cognitive ability, something that is also highly valuable in the labour market.[28]

Our preference for status is not that much different from our preference for employing or dating tall people. Relative standing, like height, can be seen as a signal for an individual's ability level whenever ability is not directly observable to the general public. As noted by Robert Frank:

> When there is a broad dispersion in income levels, there will generally be a strong positive correlation between individual income levels and various observable consumption goods: the size or location of one's home, the quality of one's automobile or wardrobe, the clubs to which one belongs, and so on. When an individual's ability cannot be observed directly, such observable components of his consumption bundle constitute a signal to others about his total income level, and on average, therefore, about his level of ability.[29]

And given that the structure of our primary motivation, which was shaped long ago by the forces of natural selection, is a taste for reproduction and, once reproduced, seeing to it that our children are launched in life as successfully as possible, our relentless pursuit of higher relative standing as a signal for our ability to provide for loved ones, even when it may be collectively wasteful, becomes easier to understand. By the process of natural selection, we are hard-wired with the overriding belief that the highest-ranked individual will be rewarded with the most attractive mate, and that the children of the highest-ranked individual will be better endowed with resources and skills than the children of lower-ranked individuals. We are, in other words, programmed to feel bad whenever we see other people having a better chance of finding a mate than we do, or whenever we see that our children are less well provided-for than are the children of our peers.

The status meme

So, from the perspective of evolutionary theorists, the pursuit of rank seems to make perfect sense, as it's consistent with the pursuit of rational self-interest, something that economists have a lot of sympathy for. But unlike height, which is pre-determined by our parents' genes and their ability to provide for us when we were still in our teens, status as we know it can now be fairly easily bought in the era of credit cards and bank overdrafts by a simple click of a mouse. We are now living in a society in which it has never been easier for people from low-income households to go out and buy themselves a large-screen TV, a nice car, or even (until recently) a mortgage with an attractive rate in order to 'keep up with the Joneses'. And because of this, one conjecture is that today's status may have much less to do with one's income level – which is highly correlated with one's ability in the labour market – than with one's ability to meet debt obligations, which isn't perhaps one of the things that people normally look for in a potential employee or mate.

Yet, despite the continuing decline in the real importance of status and what it stands for, our attitudes towards it remain virtually unscratched. To most of us, the pursuit of status or relative standing remains one of the most basic human motivations, regardless of whether it's still a valid proxy for one's ability level. Our refusal to let go of this overriding belief, even when it may no longer be rational even at the individual level to hold on to it, is a direct product of a 'meme', a term first used by the British evolutionary biologist Richard Dawkins to describe a transmission of ideas or behaviours from person to person within a culture, analogous to the passing down of genes (in that the ideas or behaviours are self-replicated and respond to selective pressures).[30]

So the important question is whether there's a way to go about changing or moderating such a belief when it's self-replicated and so deeply rooted within our culture. And if the pursuit of higher incomes for the sake of higher relative standing is ultimately wasteful, how much does money, when it's being given to us *exogenously* – in other words, if it's money that we didn't have to sweat blood to earn, but is instead randomly and serendipitously given to us, like lottery wins, for example – how much does this money really matter to our happiness? What are the 'other' things that make us happy, then, if money really can't? How about friendships and children? Could these two non-marketable things (i.e. not purchasable from any legally-operated markets) make us happier than, say, winning £1,000 from the National Lottery?

CHAPTER 4

THE PRICE OF WHAT MONEY CAN'T BUY: PART I

One of the most successful advertising campaigns in US and UK marketing history is the one employed by MasterCard. Their 'priceless' campaign, which has produced 160-odd commercials over the course of nine years,[1] has helped their present and potential customers to think about money in the most sentimental way possible: as a *means* to something that money itself can't really buy – be it a real conversation with our son, or an opportunity to be with the people who understand us, or even the chance to start a new life with someone we love.

The slogan, 'There are some things money can't buy. For everything else, there's MasterCard®', was created specifically to frame us to think about money – whether in the form of cash or credit – in only the most positive light, by dissociating it from the popular concern that everything in today's world is 'marketable' and that people are now too materialistic for their own good. 'See?', I can imagine the voiceover man from the adverts saying, 'Even if money can't actually buy you love, it still has the capacity to take you to all the happiness you can reap from this priceless, schmaltzy stuff.'

Let's put that to the test.

The happiness equation
When it comes to formulating happiness, our mind is like a big black box. There's an input lead of life events – as well as tangible and intangible experiences – going into it at one end and an output lead of happiness coming out at the other end. Sometimes we make spot-on predictions on the size of the

happiness multipliers within – the factors that measure how much happiness changes in response to a change in certain input variables. But most of the time we don't. In other words, what happens in the big black box really is anybody's guess.

Well, at least up until recently, anyway.

The scientific understanding of the term 'happiness equation' was perhaps popularised for the lay audience for the first time in 2006 by Andrew Oswald.[2] According to Andrew, our happiness – which has been shown in Chapter 2 to be measurable and able to be put into a numerical scale (e.g., 'How satisfied are you with your life overall?' 1 = Least satisfied, 7 = Very satisfied) – can be thought of as an output that depends on a wide range of factors. And by using normal statistical methods (of the sort used to study how smoking or eating fresh fruit and vegetables affects the chance of a long life) it's possible to examine how, for example, marriage, income and social ties affect how happy we are. More crucially, in this research it's possible to calculate the *separate* effects on happiness of being married compared to having a high income, compared to having a lot of friends, compared to becoming unemployed, and so on.

However, the process of formulating a happiness equation that is truly *causal* may not be as straightforward as one might think. For example, we may observe that married people are extremely happy with their lives, but that doesn't mean marriage will make people happy. It may just be that happy people select themselves into marriage while unhappy people don't.

The following two chapters on 'The price of what money can't buy' have this cause-and-effect issue at heart. In Part I, I will first tell you how a simple happiness equation can be formulated. What goes into it? And what's coming out from it? I will then describe the first potential pitfall – the problem of unobserved personality traits bias in confounding the 'true' effects on happiness of certain life events and experiences, and how we can correct for this. I will then use Part II to describe another potential pitfall associated with the sorting out of cause and effect in the happiness equation: the omitted variables problem. Finally, I will illustrate how we can use the true effect of money on happiness to start putting price tags on many of the things that money can't buy, including marriage, social relationships, and even children.

But first, let's have a brief look at what correlates with – but is not necessarily the cause of – people's happiness.

The happiness factors

Happiness comes from within and without. First, even when there's nothing else, there's always personality. Some of us are born with persistent personality traits that keep us on either a constant natural high or a steady path of despair. According to a meta-analysis (one that combines the results of several studies that address a set of related research hypotheses in order to arrive at a common conclusion) conducted by two psychology professors, Kristina De Neve and Harris Cooper, there are over 130 personality traits that correlate with happiness.[3] Both positively and negatively.

The authors find that people born with personality traits that can be classified either as extraversion (the opposite of introversion, e.g. excitement-seeking, sociability and assertiveness), agreeableness (e.g. affiliation, social desirability and understanding), conscientiousness (e.g. control, impulsivity and plasticity), or openness to experience (e.g. creativity, self-confidence and practicality) are more likely than others to report a very high life satisfaction or happiness score in a normal survey. But the reverse is true for those born with personality traits that can be put into the 'neuroticism' category (e.g. anger, anxiety and self-consciousness). Holding other things constant, these individuals are more likely than others to report themselves to be extremely unhappy with their lives.

And then there's (almost) everything else. Things like marriage, friendship, education, work, weather, a packet of crisps, a Mars bar. All of these can – and probably will – affect how many of us rate our personal subjective well-being when we're prompted to think about it. Whether their impacts are large enough to show up in more than one nationally representative data set at more than one time period is, however, a different issue altogether.

So, what are these 'large enough' determinants of happiness that keep popping up over and over again in different data sets?

In a recent literature review on what makes us happy by two economists, Paul Dolan of the London School of Economics and Tessa Peasgood of Imperial College London, and psychologist Mathew White of Plymouth University,[4] other than absolute and relative income (already discussed in the previous chapter), the common 'large enough' determinants of happiness include, for example: age, gender, ethnicity (*characteristics of who we are*); education, health, type of work, unemployment (*our socially developed characteristics*); hours worked, commuting, care for others, community involvement and volunteering, exercise, religious activities (*how we spend our time*); attitudes towards our circumstances, trust, political persuasion, religion (*attitudes towards self and others*); marriage and intimate relationships, seeing family and friends (*our relationships with others*); income inequality, unemployment rates, inflation, welfare system and public insurance, degree of democracy, climate and the natural environment, safety and deprivation of the area, urbanisation (*where we live*). All of these factors have been shown to correlate – either positively or negatively – with people's subjective well-being across different countries and time periods.

Now, I can imagine some of you are probably thinking – *so what*? So what if our happiness correlates positively with, say, the amount of time we spend with our friends and family? So what if unemployed people or crime victims are unhappy with their lives? Aren't many of these so-called 'scientific' findings a little too obvious to anyone with a morsel of common sense anyway?

Yes, of course. Although perhaps not all of them are as palpable as we might think.

For instance, it would seem virtually impossible for any one of us to try to guess when exactly our 'mid-life crisis' is going to start – if ever – especially if we've never experienced it ourselves. But with the help of a study conducted by David Blanchflower and Andrew Oswald, we're able to say that, empirically, subjective well-being has a pronounced U-shaped relationship with age – with higher levels of life satisfaction at the younger and older age points and the lowest life satisfaction occurring somewhere in the middle.[5] In a similar vein, they also provide supporting evidence that, on average, depression peaks at around the mid-40s (see Figure 4 for a UK example). From their amazing study covering 80 countries from all over the world, the authors have been able to show not only that there is evidence for such a thing as a mid-life crisis, but also that Switzerland has one of the lowest average ages at which life satisfaction is at the minimum, at 35.2 years, while France – *sacrebleu*! – has one of the highest, at 61.9 years.

The relationship between happiness and gender is also one that might be hard to predict. At the cross-section (i.e. data collected by observing many individuals at the same point of time), while women tend to report higher satisfaction levels

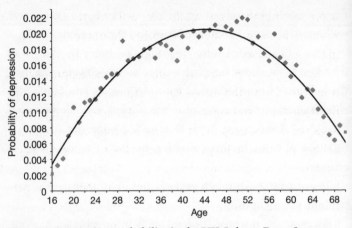

Figure 4. Depression probability in the UK, Labour Force Survey, 2004–07.

Source: Blanchflower and Oswald, 2008.

with life[6] and job[7] compared to men, they often score much worse in the positive-negative affects (or short-term emotions) questionnaires.[8] In other words, while women more than men tend to be more cognitively satisfied with their job domain as well as their overall quality of life (the kind of warm glow that is associated with their past, present and future), their day-to-day emotions tend to fluctuate a lot more than men's. However, it looks as if this satisfaction or happiness gap between men and women is closing over time. According to a recent study of the happiness of American women since the 1970s by economists Betsey Stevenson and Justin Wolfers, women's happiness has actually been declining both absolutely and relative to men over the past 35 years – despite the fact that many objective measures of the quality of women's lives (e.g. social status and pay) have been improving in the United States over that time period.[9] Undoubtedly, such a paradoxical finding of declining female happiness over the past three decades will fly in the face of many women out there who believe that they should be happier now, in this modern society, than ever before.

Another counter-intuitive finding from the happiness litera-ture comes from the mixed-bag relationship between subjec-tive well-being and education. Holding, among other things, health and income constant,[10] there is strong evidence that, in Britain, people who have completed at least a university degree tend to report significantly lower levels of job satisfaction[11] and higher levels of mental distress (a combination of, among other things, not being able to sleep, not being able to make decisions, low confidence and low self-esteem)[12] compared to those who come from a lower educational background. An additional level of education, however, seems to have a positive relationship with measures of happiness and satisfaction for people living in countries such as Switzerland,[13] the Latin American nations[14] and the US.[15] This, of course, leads to deep and important ques-tions about the 'true' impact of education upon our subjective well-being. What explains, for example, why education – after holding health and income constant – is associated negatively with some measures of subjective well-being (e.g. job satisfac-tion and mental well-being) but not others (e.g. happiness and life satisfaction)? Do different countries – and societies – value an additional level of education differently from one another? Does education raise our expectations about a particular life domain (such as our job) more than it does in other areas? Many of these thought-provoking questions about education wouldn't have been possible had it not been for the research on happiness.

The same probably holds true for career choices. Using an American data set that comprises over 52,000 participants between 1972 and 2006, survey expert Tom Smith of the

University of Chicago set out to analyse the relationship between people's career paths and their self-rated job satisfaction.[16] He produced a table of rankings of the top ten most (and least) satisfied jobs in America that might have been hard to predict.

Rank	Occupation	Mean score (4-point scale)	% Very satisfied (= 4)
Top ten			
1	Clergy	3.79	87.2
2	Physiotherapists	3.72	78.1
3	Firefighters	3.67	80.1
4	Education administrators	3.62	68.4
5	Painters, sculptors, related	3.62	67.3
6	Teachers	3.61	69.2
7	Authors	3.59	74.2
8	Psychologists	3.59	66.9
9	Special education teachers	3.56	70.1
10	Operating engineers	3.56	64.1
Bottom ten			
1	Roofers	2.84	25.3
2	Waiters/servers	2.85	27.0
3	Labourers, except construction	2.86	21.4
4	Bartenders	2.88	26.4
5	Hand packers and packagers	2.88	23.7
6	Freight, stock/material handlers	2.91	25.8
7	Apparel/clothing salesperson	2.93	23.9
8	Cashiers	2.94	25.0
9	Food preparers	2.95	23.6
10	Expediters	2.97	37.0

Figure 5.

Without having worked in every single job the American labour market has to offer, it would be virtually impossible for any of us to second-guess, for instance, which jobs would make the top five most satisfied occupations, or even the worst career path to take (notice how dentistry didn't even make the top ten least likeable jobs), for the American people over the past three decades.

People are also fascinated by, and enjoy, sex. But without the study that examined the link between happiness and sex,[17] how would we have known that (i) there's little evidence that men enjoy sex slightly more than women; (ii) sex may bring more happiness to the highly educated (university degree-level) than to the less-educated; (iii) people who practise monogamy are, on average, significantly happier compared to those who have sex with multiple partners; and (iv) homosexuality has no significant effect – positive or negative – on happiness?

But rather than summarise every known factor in the literature that has been found to correlate with our subjective well-being,[18] it's perhaps more fundamentally important to focus on the following two rarely addressed questions. How many of these observed correlations with happiness – age, gender, education, or even career choices – are actually *causal*, with an effect that clearly runs from one direction to the other? And, more crucially, how 'large' are these so-called effects?

Before we do this, let's just look at why we have to care so much about cause and effect. Can we not just pretend that any observed relationship between happiness and a life event is causal and be done with it?

There are actually many real-world examples and much anecdotal evidence showing why distinctions between correlation and causation are of the utmost importance to all social scientists, not just happiness researchers. Many observable things in our lives are correlated – the number of fire engines and the damage caused by all the fires in a city, cigarette consumption and lower grades in college, educational attainment and the number of books a child has at home – but are unlikely to be causally related.[19] Statisticians call these types of association 'spurious correlations'. And this can be explained by the fact that there may well be some third, unknown variable that simultaneously correlates with the two variables in question. For instance, consider the following newspaper headline: 'Bottled Water Linked to Healthier Babies'. Now, for parents-to-be, this might have a hugely positive effect on their subsequent bottled water consumption. But does the headline really mean what it says? Can drinking bottled water every day really lead to parents having healthier and stronger babies?

Maybe.

Yet it really could just be that more affluent parents are more likely than others to have healthier babies simply because their living standards are higher. Additionally, they are also more likely to spend money on bottled water, which is not a necessity but slightly luxurious, than parents who are less affluent, for example.[20] In other words, without giving further consideration to other relevant variables such as parental income, this headline should be interpreted with plenty of caution. This is simply because there may well be no linkage at all between drinking bottled water and parents giving birth to healthier babies when income is held constant across all parents-to-be.

Not only could misinterpreting a correlation as cause and effect be potentially costly (think of the amount of bottled water that could be sold with that kind of headline), it could also be extremely embarrassing. During a live nationwide TV interview of the candidates for mayor of Bangkok in 2008, one of the candidates was seen answering a question on what the new mayor could do to improve the educational attainment of inner-city kids.

'Put more salt in their diet,' he said.

'Why?' The interviewer was obviously puzzled by his remark.

According to the wannabe mayor, low intelligence quotient (IQ) is often observed with low salt intake. So, he concluded, salt must cause intelligence. In reality, of course, it may be the case that children from more affluent households have more intelligent parents – the father's and mother's levels of education are two of the main factors that determine kids' IQ – as well as a diet richer in salt than children from less affluent households.

Imagine the long-term impact on their health of a substantial increase in salt intake, if he did win the election.

The art of identification

So how do we relate the spurious correlation problem to the study of happiness? If we see somebody who's rich and happy, does that mean more money buys happiness? What about somebody who has a lot of friends saying that she's very satisfied with life? Does that imply that friendship improves her life for the better?

If only things were that simple.

Imagine two friends, Richard and Robert. A natural-born confident person, Richard leaves his home every morning feeling like a world-beater, as if he can do no wrong. He also works harder than anybody else in his workplace – simply because he believes he can – and, consequently, earns himself higher wages in the process. And being the high-self-esteemed person he is, he also likes to tick the 'Very satisfied' box whenever he's asked to report how satisfied he is with his life overall.

His mate Robert, by contrast, was born with personality traits that constantly keep him on a low stock of self-assurance. He hates getting up for work every morning, and when he eventually gets there he makes no effort to hide the fact that he's not really too sure of what he's doing with his job. As a result, he earns relatively less than his fellow workers – simply because he's not as productive. And being the low-self-esteemed person he is, he also tends to tick the 'Very dissatisfied' box whenever he's asked to report how satisfied he is with his life overall.

To an untrained eye, an observation of both Richard's and Robert's income levels and self-reported life satisfaction scores might automatically lead to the conclusion that money buys happiness – when it really could just be that Richard's personality traits (which are generally unobservable to anyone who doesn't know him personally) make him more productive in the workplace, as well as making him a lot happier with life in general, compared to Robert's.

But that doesn't mean, of course, that money *doesn't* buy happiness. It just means that we can't say for sure that it does.

That's all.

Further to this, how do we know for certain that causality doesn't run in the other direction – i.e., from happiness to income? Independent from his cheerful personality, how can we be so sure that a happier Richard today compared to himself from yesterday wouldn't put in more effort and earn himself higher pay in the process?[21]

To establish how something is causally linked with our well-being is perhaps one of the most important objectives in the study of happiness. Yet getting around the above identification problems can be a tough, sometimes messy business.[22] The process involves, for example, separating out the effects of our personality traits in influencing both how our life is turning out objectively – e.g. how much we earn, the type of job we're in, how frequently we see our friends – and how we rate how happy we are in a survey. Occasionally, it requires finding a variable that correlates with our objective circumstances but not with our happiness. This so-called 'instrumental variable' approach allows researchers to estimate how much X affects Y by making use of the additional information provided by variable Z, which affects Y only through Z's effect on X.

What's that in simple English, you might say.

Allow me to explain it better by breaking things down into smaller, digestible chunks. Suppose we want to find out how much schooling affects our satisfaction with life overall when we're in our 40s. Our first step, then, is to come up with plausible theories to support why schooling should be related to our overall happiness. For instance, there's plenty of evidence to suggest that more schooling helps improve our expected lifetime earnings[23] and later health (such as improved blood pressure),[24] which could then reflect in an increase in our satisfaction with life overall. By contrast, it may also be the case that people who are born happy may choose to stay in school for longer, on average, compared to the unhappy ones who decide to quit school early. Because of these contradicting hypotheses, the extent of the overall effect of schooling on life satisfaction is assumed to be unclear on *a priori* ground.

Having identified the potential reverse causality problem between schooling and life satisfaction, we can then move on to the second step of our identification strategy. One way of dealing with this – as mentioned above – is to find a good instrumental variable that directly affects our schooling decision but not our overall life satisfaction in our 40s.

Economics professor Philip Oreopoulos of the University of Toronto, who has devoted almost his entire academic career to the study of the causal effect of schooling on various different life outcomes such as wages and health, proposes that we can use a change in the nationwide education law as our instrument for schooling. The example he gives is the introduction of ROSLA

(Raising of School-Leaving Age) policy in the UK whereby, after the year 1947, no student under the age of fourteen could leave full-time education.[25] His idea is extremely simple: a change in the minimum school-leaving age from fourteen to fifteen in the UK in 1947 affected the schooling decision only of those who were exposed to it, while there's no reason to believe that such a change in the law would have direct implications upon these individuals' life satisfaction later on in life. This makes it possible for us to compare the average life satisfaction of two groups of individuals: those who were randomly exposed to the old compulsory schooling law prior to 1947 (i.e. the control group), and those who were randomly exposed to the new compulsory schooling law from 1947 onwards (i.e. the treated group). Since people in the treated group would have had no choice but to remain at school for one extra year, as opposed to those in the control group who always had the choice of leaving school one year early, the average number of years spent in formal education is likely to be higher in the former group than in the latter. And, more importantly, because this one extra year of schooling was imposed upon the individuals in the treated group in an exogenous manner – that is, the decision on whether or not to quit school early was completely out of their hands – any differences in the average life satisfaction scores between the two groups can be interpreted as the *causal* effect of schooling on life satisfaction.[26] It's that easy.

But now imagine trying to find suitable instrumental variables for each and every life event that strikes our interest. It becomes virtually impossible to do, for a simple reason.

While it may seem morally acceptable for any government to introduce an educational policy that would give a random group of students an extra year of education, it would be viewed as extremely unethical to force a random group of single people to marry simply because we want to estimate the causal effect of marriage on happiness, for example.

So, perhaps the best that we can do is try to work with what we've got first. Unlike the reverse causality issue (the effect running from happiness to the happening of the event of interest), the personality traits conundrum is relatively easier to deal with, provided we have a large longitudinal data set that keeps a good track of the same individuals repeatedly over time.

And this is how it works.

Going back to our two friends, Richard and Robert, let's imagine that, having met them both outside their homes one weekday morning, we begin following them over the course of the next ten years or so. During which time, we also observe almost every detail about their lives, including, but not limited to, whether they're married, employed full-time, how much salary they get per annum, how many children they are raising in the household, how often they see their friends on a daily basis, and also how happy or satisfied with life they are. We also do the same pestering routine for 9,998 other randomly-selected individuals in different areas around the country.

Once all the information has been gathered and combined to form a single, longitudinal data set, all we need to do to eliminate these 10,000 individuals' personality traits is to 'time-demean' everything from their reported happiness to their objective personal characteristics that include, but are not limited to, their income, employment status and marital status.

Time-demean, in this particular case, is a statistical terminology meaning 'to keep only within-person variation'. This is done by subtracting from the data set all of the between-person differences that don't change over time. These include people's unobserved personality traits and their stable social environment, both of which are likely to be time-invariant but vary from person to person.[27]

To illustrate how this works, let's imagine that there exists a happiness equation of the following form:

$$\text{Happiness}_{i,t} = \beta \times \text{Income}_{i,t} + \text{Personality}_i + \text{Error term}_{i,t}$$

Here, happiness is assumed for simplicity to be determined by three things: our income levels, our personality, and what can be generalised as the 'error term' (this could be everything else that's related to happiness *plus* our inability to communicate our 'true' well-being accurately). The subscripts i and t are there to help us identify each relevant *individual* and *time period* in the data set, i.e., they are not parameters that will be calculated as part of the equation. If there are 10,000 individuals and ten years' worth of information in the annually-collected data set, the individual subscript i will range from 1 to 10,000 and the time subscript t will range from 1 to 10. The term β (beta) denotes how much happiness can be raised from a one-unit change in the income variable; more will be said about this a little later on.

To see how happiness data and other relevant information are normally collected and organised, let's imagine that a man came over to your house one afternoon in 1991 asking to conduct an interview with you and your girlfriend about the many aspects of your lives in exchange for a small fee. Despite feeling rather reluctant at first, you and your girlfriend finally agreed to the interview – provided that the information you gave would always remain anonymous to those who used it. He then surveyed you about your job, your education, your earnings, your general happiness with the life you lead. He gave you a unique personal identification number (say, 2325) and then repeated the same questions to your girlfriend (her personal number, for the sake of consistency, is 2326). Once finished, he packed up his laptop, finished his cup of tea, scheduled his next interview with you, said thank you and left. He then repeated the routine every year for the next five years or so.

In his laptop, there is five years' worth of data on happiness and income that looks something like this:

Personal identification (i)	Time (t), i.e. 1991 = 1	Happiness (7-point score)	Annual income
2325	1	4	£35,344
2325	2	6	£36,299
2325	3	5	£36,750
2325	4	5	£37,800
2325	5	4	£38,323
2326	1	6	£56,000
2326	2	5	£58,432
2326	3	5	£61,478
2326	4	7	£62,390
2326	5	5	£62,700

Figure 6.

Does money buy you and your girlfriend happiness? A quick look at the raw information seems to suggest 'Yes!' A simple scatter plot of happiness and income of paired data, using only five years of observations from you and your girlfriend (i.e. ten observations) yields a positive relationship between annual income (in £1,000s) and self-rated happiness on average. And this can be shown by simply drawing a line that best fits the data, as shown in Figure 7, where the triangles represent you at five different time periods and the squares represent your girlfriend, again at five different time periods.

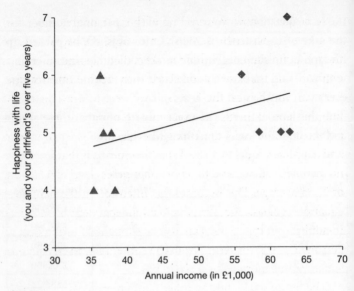

Figure 7.

And this is where our happiness equation comes in. Your happiness in 1991 (which you reported as 4 here) is assumed to be an outcome of (or determined by) your corresponding income at the same time period. It's also determined by your personality traits that don't change over time but that, unfortunately, were unobservable to the researcher during the interview. The same applies for subsequent years, and also for your girlfriend. Average all the data points together and we have ourselves a merry equation.

So, with only five years' worth of data points between you and your girlfriend, our tenable happiness equation would look something like this:

$$\text{Happiness}_{i,t} = 0.033 \times \text{Income}_{i,t} + 3.589$$

At a glance, how we come up with these figures may seem daunting to non-mathematicians. However, the way we derive them is quite simple. The diagram says that happiness, which is on the Y-axis, is positively correlated with income (measured in £1,000s), which is on the X-axis. If we were to draw a straight line that cuts through the exact middle point of these scatter points, it would cross the Y-axis when income is equal to zero and happiness equal to 3.589. What that means is that if we have no income at all, we tend to report a happiness level of 3.589 out of 7, on average. This becomes the 'intercept' in the happiness equation (or basically our happiness independent of income). In addition to this, 3.589 can also be thought of as the sum of Personality$_i$ + Error term$_{i,t}$ from the earlier happiness equation which, at this moment, is inseparable.

The figure 0.033, on the other hand, represents the average relationship between money and happiness experienced by you and your girlfriend. Visually, it represents the slope (or steepness) of the straight line on the graph, i.e., if we start moving along the straight line to the right by £1,000, the corresponding increase in terms of happiness on the Y-axis would be 0.033 out of 7, on average. In other words, it's the change in the values on the Y-axis divided by the change in the values on the X-axis.

If, for every unit increase in income (one unit here is measured in £1,000 on the diagram) our happiness goes up by 0.033 on average, then the slope is 0.033/1 = 0.033. In other words, what the diagram is implying is that a £1,000 increase in annual income is associated, on average, with a 0.033 increase in the happiness score (measured on a 7-point scale). This figure 0.033, denoted generally as β in the original happiness equation, can be thought of as our income coefficient – or, basically, an indicator of how much income is correlated with our happiness, all else being equal.

So, given the above happiness equation, we can now provide simple answers to questions like: 'How much would £57,000 buy in terms of happiness?' Provided that a £1,000 increase in income is associated with a 0.033 increase in the happiness score, then £57,000 would buy us 57 × 0.033 = 1.8 happiness score.

One natural objection is that this estimated correlation between income and happiness is not causal. As mentioned earlier, the observed link between happiness and income may not represent a real relationship at all if people who are born with certain personality traits are also (i) more productive in the labour market, and (ii) more likely to report themselves as happy in surveys. If these personality traits – e.g. extraversion and agreeableness – were to be taken into account and held constant across all individuals in the estimation of the happiness–income relationship, then it might be possible that the correlation between income and happiness – our income coefficient – will be zero.

In other words, there may well be *no* relationship whatsoever between happiness and income once everybody's personality traits have been taken into account. And if that's the case, then the conventional notion that money buys happiness is nothing more than a simple case of mistaken identity: it's just that happier people earn more income, on average, than less happy people. That's all.

But given that personality traits aren't always readily observable in surveys (it's catastrophically time-consuming to objectively measure all of someone's personality traits every year for ten years), they can't be incorporated into the estimation and any relationship between self-rated happiness and income is likely to be biased, if not entirely spurious.

The time-demeaning process allows the value of each variable in the happiness equation at each different time period to be subtracted by their within-person averages. So, from the happiness equation above, the time-demeaned equation would look something like this:

$$\text{Happiness}_{i,t} - \overline{\text{Happiness}_i}$$
$$= \beta \times (\text{Income}_{i,t} - \overline{\text{Income}_i}) + (\text{Error term}_{i,t} - \overline{\text{Error term}_i})$$

Here, the barred variables represent the variables' corresponding within-person averages. Assuming that personality traits remain constant over time, the Personality_i variable disappears completely from the equation. Hence, the time-demeaning process allows us to factor out the respondents' personality traits from contaminating the relationships between other variables in the happiness equation. And a positive income coefficient here denotes the relationship between a year-to-year change in income and a corresponding year-to-year change in happiness for an average person that is independent from personality traits, as well as everything else that is unobservable and that doesn't vary over time.

And here's how we do it. Working with the same limited number of observations as before, we can see that your average happiness score over five years would be $(4 + 6 + 5 + 5 + 4)/5 = 4.8$, while your girlfriend's is 5.6 – so, on average, she's generally a lot happier than you. On the other hand, your average income over five years would be $(£35,344 + £36,299 + £36,750 + £37,800 + £38,323)/5 = £36,903$, and your girlfriend's is £60,200. And so, for 1991 (i.e., $t = 1$), your time-demeaned happiness and income are $(4 - 4.8) = -0.8$ and $(£35,344 - £36,903) = -£1,559$. What this implies is that, in 1991, you are slightly less happy compared to what you 'usually' are, while earning less money than you 'usually' earn. Do the same for the rest of the observations and we get the results shown in Figure 8.

Personal identification (i)	Time (t), i.e. 1991 = 1	Time-demeaned happiness (7-point score)	Time-demeaned annual income
2325	1	−0.8	−£1,559
2325	2	1.2	−£604
2325	3	0.2	−£153
2325	4	0.2	£897
2325	5	−0.8	£1,420
2326	1	0.4	−£4,200
2326	2	−0.6	−£1,768
2326	3	−0.6	£1,278
2326	4	1.4	£2,190
2326	5	−0.6	£2,500

Figure 8.

Plot the time-demeaned happiness scores against the time-demeaned income levels and we can see that the previously observed positive correlation between money and happiness completely disappears. The slope of the best line of fits (or the income coefficient) is now a mere −0.001. (See Figure 9.)

Once we account for the unobserved differences between your personality traits and your girlfriend's personality traits, money doesn't seem to be correlated with happiness at all. (Again, the triangles represent you at five different time periods and the squares represent your girlfriend at five different time periods.)

But of course, the above is based only on the ten observations of you and your girlfriend between 1991 and 1995, which is hardly representative of everyone living in the UK during that period. More data points of people across different socio-demographics (the old, the young, the employed, the retired, southerners, northerners, and so on) are needed for us to estimate an income coefficient that is nationally representative.

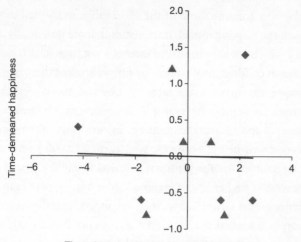

Figure 9.

And provided that we have a nationally representative sample of everyone in the UK to hand, and that the last term in our happiness equation, (Error term$_{i,t}$ − $\overline{\text{Error term}_i}$), doesn't correlate with the respondent's income – i.e., there are no other omitted time-varying factors that make us earn more (or less) while, at the same time, making us happier (or unhappier), so that the income effect is pure and bias-free from these omitted influences – we can interpret the income coefficient as capturing the 'true' or causal effect of income on happiness for an average individual in the UK. In other words, if the unobserved personality traits bias is the only factor biasing the happiness–income relationship, then time-demeaning the data alone should be sufficient to get an estimate of how much money really matters to us.

But that's just wishful thinking, of course.

For one thing, it's pretty unlikely that income is uncorrelated with any other time-varying variables that may have been omitted from the actual estimation. While it may be possible for us to take into account some of the observable, individual differences in the respondents' characteristics that are potentially correlated with both happiness and income – e.g., age, health status, number of children, profession – by simply holding them fixed in the happiness equation, the same can't be said about everything else that's not readily observable in these surveys. Remember the previous chapter about the impact of income rank in the society upon our well-being? Someone who earns £20,000 a year may well be happier than someone who earns £50,000 a year if the former ranks higher in the income ladder among people in his reference group. Given that we may not always have the information on income rank readily available (it seems difficult to gather this kind of information in normal household surveys), then it's likely to be the case that the size of the income coefficient is going to be biased towards zero. The same problem applies with everything else that correlates with both income and happiness, but that can't be easily controlled for when it comes to estimating how much happiness is related to income.

In other words, by omitting other people's incomes in our estimation of the happiness–income relationship, there will be an illusion that income doesn't matter as much as it should, simply because rich people living in an even richer neighbourhood are no happier than poor people living in a poorer neighbourhood. And unless we can control for everything that income is correlated with, the happiness–income relationship is subject to be biased with *a priori* unknown directions and magnitudes.

Secondly, the time-demeaning process works only with variables that are time-varying. Hence, things that do not or hardly change over time – education is a prime example – will likely disappear following the process of time-demeaning. What this means is that we will not be able to find a causal effect of a time-invariant factor on happiness using this approach.

How much does money really matter?

But all is not lost. The random nature of some life events means that, after the time-demeaning process, we can perhaps interpret their relationships with happiness as causal. Take deaths of loved ones[28] and disabilities,[29] for example. As grim as they are, these life events can perhaps be taken as exogenous – they occur randomly across the population. The case is even stronger after the time-demeaning process, as people may argue that individuals born with persistent personalities that make them unhappy are more likely to commit suicide or take extraordinarily harmful risks that can result in death or disabilities. And so, after we have time-demeaned the data and included sufficient controls on some of the respondents' socio-demographic statuses such as health and employment, it would be perfectly reasonable to interpret any relationship between happiness and death of loved ones (or happiness and disabilities) as causal.

How about money? Unfortunately, money just doesn't fall within the 'exogenous' category. It may be true that people born with personality traits that keep them happy tend to earn more, on average. But how much we earn in a year may also depend on a whole list of other factors that can vary over time. Things like job expectations and the location of our workplace, for example. If we aren't able to keep these variables constant across everyone in the sample, then the happiness–income relationship will be biased, too. In other words, the time-demeaning approach can help us get closer to estimating the pure income effect on happiness, but not close enough for a cigar.

So how do we do it, then? How do we go about estimating the purest form of income effect on happiness when there are so many things – other than our inborn predispositions – that are potentially correlated with both income and happiness?

CHAPTER 5

THE PRICE OF WHAT MONEY CAN'T BUY: PART II

Perhaps one of the most important questions in social science, 'How much does money *really* buy happiness?', also happens to be one of the most intricate problems that economists ever have to solve. Easterlin Paradox aside, the reason for this is simple: an instrumental variable that affects our incomes directly but not our happiness is painfully difficult to find. But there have been a few reasonable efforts in recent years to try to establish the causal effect of income on happiness.

One notable attempt to solve the happiness–income relationship conundrum was carried out by Andrew Oswald and Jonathan Gardner of the University of Warwick.[1] Together, they conducted a study on the impact of winning a lottery on mental health in Britain.[2] A study of lottery winners is particularly interesting because the winning amount is entirely random among those who play and win. More specifically, there's no reason to believe that happier people are more likely to win higher amounts than others, on average.

What Oswald and Gardner found from their analysis of lottery winners probably came as a total surprise to both of them. Among those who took part and won, there was no evidence whatsoever of improved mental health in the year of winning at least £1,000 ($1,500) from the lottery. On the contrary, they found that people actually became significantly more stressed in the year of winning. The hit on mental well-being, however, came in the third year; lottery winners eventually became a lot happier two years after winning a pot of at least £1,000.

So there seems to be a delayed effect on improved mental health following a lottery win. Lottery money buys happiness, but not in the first year of winning it – which, on the surface, seems highly counter-intuitive. Corroborative evidence is obtained using a German data set whereby other measures of well-being – e.g. happiness and life satisfaction – are used instead of the respondent's self-reported mental health status.[3]

But why is that? What explains why it takes so long for winners to gain satisfaction from their windfall? According to a recent longitudinal study of lottery winners in Germany, one plausible explanation for this may lie in the natural difference between earned income and lottery wins. On the one hand, earned income is seen by the person as money that she intrinsically deserves (I put in the hours for it, therefore I'm going to enjoy it). A lottery win, on the other hand, isn't viewed in the same way. Because winning is serendipitous, the individual may not think immediately that she fully 'deserves' the money.[4] Until she comes to terms with the win, there's a kind of psychic 'tax' imposed on the win itself. Admittedly, however, this is only a conjecture.

The idea that a lottery win doesn't buy us instant happiness goes completely against what ticket buyers hold dear to their hearts – the prospect of being rich *and* happy beyond their wildest dreams if they win a bit of cash. But that's what the data say. And it's hard to argue against hard numbers when they can be replicated across different samples and measures of well-being.

So how much can money from a lottery win buy us in terms of happiness at the third year of winning? In terms of mental health, a win of at least £1,000 will help improve our mental well-being by approximately 15 percentage points (or 1.8 points on the 12-point scale of the General Health Questionnaire (GHQ-12) measure of mental health). Is that big? Well, it's roughly six times the effect of getting married on mental well-being.

So, yes; unless you were forced into marrying someone you didn't particularly want to marry, it's pretty darn big. An exogenous increase in our absolute income levels through winning a lottery *does* buy us a significant level of happiness. Or so it seems.

But, unfortunately, we can't generalise this finding by saying that a positive shock in earnings would buy a lot of happiness for everyone in a population, for the simplest of reasons. And that's because the sample of lottery winners is unlikely to be representative of an average person in a population. Money may buy a lot of happiness for these lottery winners. Yet, because people who play the lottery (and win) make up only a tiny fraction of the people in any given country, it seems presumptuous to conclude that money will also buy a lot of happiness for the average individual in that nation.

So I guess it's back to the drawing board, then.

While lottery winners make for a very interesting case study, more evidence is needed to make the 'money can really buy happiness' claim convincing beyond reasonable doubt. The problem is how to find some kind of exogenous (or random) shock in income that affects virtually everyone in a population sample.

In the early months of 2003, three economists, Paul Frijters, Michael Shields and John Haisken-DeNew, decided to take on the challenge of trying to identify the causal effect of income on happiness that would be representative at a national level.[5] And what was the trick up their sleeves? It was the reunification of East and West Germany in 1990.

It all began with the falling of the Berlin Wall, which started in the late evening of 9 November 1989 and ended with an officially signed German unity treaty on 3 October 1990. Shortly after the historic and unanticipated press release by a spokesman of the Politburo leader Egon Krenz allowing East Berliners to travel freely through crossing points between East Germany (the poor and failing economy in the Soviet zones of occupation) and West Germany (the rich and prospering economy in the Allied zones of occupation), the wall fell. This led to a large influx of East Germans crossing into West Berlin for the first time since before the end of the Second World War, all seeking a better life in the thriving economy of West Germany. Moreover, the falling of the Berlin Wall also led to a radical change in the economic environment and conditions in East Germany. For one thing, savings were increased in real terms overnight. There were also significant increases in terms of wages demanded by East German workers compared to the period before the fall of the wall and, consequently, many jobs in industry and government were suddenly much higher-paid than before.[6]

Because the fall of the Berlin Wall is widely acknowledged to have been completely unanticipated, and since it resulted in large income transfers to virtually all of the population of East Germany, it was literally like every East German person winning a lottery without having to buy a ticket. The widespread positive income shock also carried with it a great deal of random individual variation. For instance, civil servants in the years immediately following reunification obtained similar wages to their colleagues in West Germany, but many individuals in other industries did not.

Realising that the falling of the Berlin Wall was an amazingly large-scale 'natural experiment',[7] the three economists set out to investigate what happened to the life satisfaction – normally used to measure people's well-being that is more cognitively than emotionally driven[8] – of East Germans following

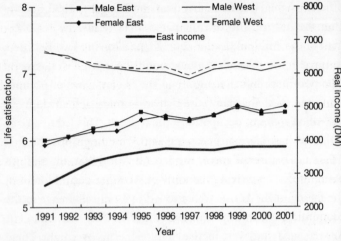

Figure 10. The relationship between the change in aggregate life satisfaction and the change in average real household monthly income (in 1995 prices) experienced by East German males and females over the period 1991 to 2001. There is a clear positive relationship between income and aggregate life satisfaction for East Germans during this period, while there is no sign of West Germans getting any happier with life in the same period.

Source: Frijters, Shields and Haisken-DeNew, 2004.

the big increase in real incomes immediately after reunification in 1990. By following the same East German males and females from 1991 for eleven years, they found that, on average, a 1-percentage-point increase in real household income led to around a 0.5-point increase in the 11-point scale of life satisfaction (0 = Very dissatisfied; 10 = Very satisfied) for both men and women. And how large is this? Well, it's equivalent to the effect of moving from unemployment to full-time employment, which is pretty massive considering that unemployment is extremely detrimental to our mental well-being *regardless* of how much income we have when we become unemployed.[9]

This is, by a long way, one of the biggest finds in the economics of happiness of recent years (a fact reflected in the findings' eventual publication in the *American Economic Review*, arguably the most prestigious economic journal in the world). For the first time, there was a general feel of exactly how much an exogenous increase in our incomes could actually buy us in terms of happiness.

Yet what are the chances that this finding applies only to East Germans and nowhere else? Can we generalise the three economists' results across different countries and economic environments? And to what extent is this causal estimate of the happiness–income relationship different from its non-causal counterpart?

Well, I suppose Germany's footballing best friend – the British public – is as good a place as any to start replicating the East German results. But naturally it's almost always the case that whenever we switch our analysis to another country and another population sample altogether, we risk running into that same old identification problem again. And, unlike Germany, there's unfortunately no equivalent falling of a wall of any kind for us to experiment with in Britain. Thus, a completely new identification strategy has to be thought up from scratch.

Recalling the instrumental variable approach, a causal effect of income on happiness can be identified if we can somehow find a variable that is correlated with our income but not with our happiness, conditional on other things in our happiness equation being equal. Well, if that's the case, then how about the information on payslips as a potential instrumental variable for income?[10]

In one well-known longitudinal British data set (the British Household Panel Survey or BHPS),[11] there's a wonderful and seemingly unrelated variable that not many people have thought about before when trying to establish the causal link between income and happiness; that is, the information on whether or not the interviewer has seen the respondent's payslip. Now, as arbitrary as that may sound (how on earth can we use the information about someone's payslip to solve the almost impossible identification problem between money and happiness?), the variable holds an important key to unlocking the income effect, at least in the UK.

So how does it do it?

Well, let's first take a look at the properties of what we mean by a payslip. In Britain, a payslip is a piece of paper usually issued by an employer, typically containing information on gross income and all taxes and any other deductions such as retirement plan contributions, insurance, garnishments, or charitable contributions taken out of the gross amount to arrive at the final net pay.

And so, whenever the payslip is shown to the interviewer, the information gathered about the survey respondents' household incomes is likely to be much more accurate, thereby significantly reducing any measurement error problems associated with the recording of incomes (for example, people may misreport their incomes on purpose for social desirability reasons). In other words, there should be a direct correlation between people showing their payslip and their true household income levels. Now, while the omitted variables problem – already discussed with regard to personality and any other variables that cannot be readily included into the estimation process – and the measurement error problem denote two separate issues in causal analysis, they actually form two sides of the same coin. And this can be explained by the fact that, for both problems, there is an unaccounted-for relationship between income and the error term in the happiness equation that, if left uncorrected-for, would render the estimate useless for causal inference (remember personality trait bias?). Given that there's no reason to believe that the survey respondent's life satisfaction would be affected by whether or not the interviewer sees the payslip, we might have ourselves a valid instrumental variable – i.e., one that correlates with income but not directly with our happiness – that could help us identify the causal effect of income on happiness.

By applying this identification strategy to the British sample, the following have been uncovered:

(i) Removing individuals' personality traits altogether from the happiness equation *reduces* the overall size of the estimated correlation between income and life satisfaction. So, as anticipated, people who are born with personality traits that make them happy tend to earn significantly more income than others, on average.

(ii) But, after instrumentation,[12] it seems that money really *does* buy a lot more happiness than was implied after removing the personality bias from the happiness equation. The estimated 'real' effect of an increase in income on our happiness, arrived at through removing personality traits and by instrumentation in a longitudinal setting, is in fact *a lot larger* than what is normally observed in cross-sectional data sets, i.e., data sets that compare different individuals at one particular point of time. In other words, money really does buy happiness!

* * *

'Wait. Can I just stop you there for a moment?'

I was halfway through my lecture on the economics of happiness, which I had been invited to deliver by a positive psychologist,[13] Nash Popovic, at the University of East London. The audience was made up mostly of mature students who were studying for a Master's degree in positive psychology, many of whom, though extremely nice and extra-attentive, were tough cookies and awfully hard to please. On the big screen, the title of the slide read: 'The Causal Effect of Income on Happiness'. It was roughly the 27th time I had been stopped mid-sentence that afternoon.

'So you're telling us that the causal effect of a £1,000 increase in real household income on happiness is, what, around 0.04 on the 7-point life satisfaction scale. But, to be honest with you, that doesn't make much sense to me. Now, I'm not saying that I don't believe that you got 0.04 instead of 0.0007 or whatever' – *phew* – 'but that doesn't tell me anything useful at all. I really have no idea, for a start, how large that effect is. Do I suddenly become extremely happy with my life, when, prior to getting this extra income, I was merely content with it? Do you see what I mean?'

I smiled broadly. This is indeed a tough question, but one that I have been asked before. And it's a good thing, too, that I'm more than well prepared for it.

But before that, before I give any of my answers away, cue Professor Andrew Oswald.

Putting price tags on everything

Born in Scotland and raised in Australia, Andrew Oswald is considered a bit of an economics maverick. He began his academic career in the late 1970s doing mostly lone theoretical studies of trade unions and their roles in wage determinations,[14] but he soon expanded to radical research combining insights from psychology with traditional economic principles, such as the implications of jealousy[15] and the fact that we tend to compare ourselves with our peers and relevant others[16] in the modelling of economic behaviours.

Today, however, Andrew Oswald is probably best known for his work on the economics of happiness and his prolific relationship with the press. 'Dr Doom' – a satirical nickname given to him by Ashley Seager, a journalist at the *Guardian*, for Andrew's view on the unsustainable rise in UK house prices in the early 2000s[17] – has been popularising the idea that we can actually put price tags on our happiness for over a decade now.

I remember him describing to me in detail his method of placing a monetary value on, well, almost anything you can think of. 'The idea is simple. Say I'm assessing, on a scale of 1 to 10, how happy I feel. Perhaps I give an answer of 7. Then, let's imagine that I'm given $10,000 out of the blue – maybe from an unexpected pay rise – and next time I'm observed in happiness surveys to give the answer of 8. That gives the statistical investigator a little bit of information about me. Now imagine that my marriage breaks up, and I'm observed to drop my happiness score to a 5. That's a little more information. Or consider what happens if there's some external bad event, like a sharp rise in inflation that depresses me. All these movements in happiness scores contain valuable information.

'As you know, one individual alone doesn't provide much that's useful, partly because he or she may be going through lots of other events in life, or simply changing mood, in ways the investigator cannot easily observe. However, if we average across individuals, it's possible to learn a great deal about the forces that bear on human happiness.

'So, think of a linear happiness equation with lots of things determining the left-hand side variable; the marginal impact of each life factor upon happiness is then assessed by reading off its coefficient on the right-hand side of the happiness equation.

'Imagine that money makes people happy – preferring more income to less income, on average. In principle, then, it's possible to calculate, by seeing how much higher on the happiness score sheet a person marks when he or she gets more cash, *how much extra income would have to be given to the person to compensate exactly (neither too much nor too little) for any bad occurrence in life*. That amount of cash can be thought of as a measure of the unpleasantness of the event.

'Equivalently, good events – falling in love and getting married, say – can be studied. Then, to work out how valuable in a deep happiness sense such an event is to a person, we determine statistically how much money would have to be taken out of a person's salary cheque to keep him or her as happy as before the good event.'[18]

When I first had the methodology described to me, it all sounded so simple; too simple, in fact. Basically, all we need to do in order to calculate the monetary value of something is to work out the ratios between how much money buys happiness and how badly (or well) our lives are affected by some other external factors. Although the method is uncomplicated and takes little effort to work through, it has – like many other great, simple ideas before it – imperative practical implications. And here are just a few of them.

First, the method enables comprehensive comparisons to be made across life events with relative ease. One reason for this is that, when prompted to make any kind of comparison, it's always more practical to convert the things we wish to compare into the same metric – whether it's the heights between two buildings, the distances between two towns, the durations between two flights, or the prices between two goods. Since happiness scores aren't yet a standard metric that many people can readily relate to, happiness impacts measured in currency format seem a perfectly sensible thing to do.

Second, the method allows researchers to calculate the monetary values of non-marketable goods (or bads) – life experiences that cannot be bought or sold in the marketplace, such as friendship, good health, or even death – in a straightforward manner. And even if one might argue that there's no real need for the shadow prices for these life events to be calculated, simply because there are no markets where these goods are purchasable, their estimated monetary values still tell us a great deal about the relative importance of all these things to an average person. In addition, given that money plays a very important role in making us happy – at least in our own minds – it seems perfectly sensible to weigh the welfare impacts of 'everything else' against how much happiness money can buy us anyway.

The third implication, and perhaps the most important of all, is that the method makes it possible for us to calculate compensation variations for different kinds of life experiences in a *scientific* manner – rather than basing them simply on heuristics or 'rules of thumb'. These numbers can then be used by judges,[19] health practitioners,[20] environmentalists[21] and policy-makers[22] to better guide many of their decisions that are likely to have important consequences for people's well-being. For example, judges have often awarded financial settlements to victims in tort cases that are in practice so small that their intellectual basis is perplexing. In *West and Son vs. Shephard* (1964) in the UK, the claimant was a married woman who was 41 when severely injured. She was left paralysed in all limbs and unable to speak. A lump-sum award of £17,500 (approximately $26,250) for loss of amenity (over and above a settlement for harm to her earnings) was upheld by the House of Lords. Adjusting for inflation, that's about 5 per cent of the lifetime income for a successful professional white-collar worker today. It seems implausible that people would contentedly accept complete paralysis in return for a tiny pay rise. So, why not measure the true 'hedonic damages' – damages awarded to the plaintiff for the loss of joy of living – for these bad occurrences in life if we can?

And on that note, let me illustrate the shadow prices of different good and bad life experiences – in particular, social relationships, death and disability (in other words, the kind of experiences that can't easily be bought or sold in the market-place) – upon our happiness.

Social relationships

There's a consensus among happiness researchers that social relationships matter a great deal to our well-being. In his best-selling book *Happiness: Lessons from the New Science*, English economist Richard Layard ranks social relationships – e.g. marriage and social interactions with friends – top of the list of external factors that positively influence human happiness.[23] In *Bowling Alone: the Collapse and Revival of American Community*, Harvard sociologist Robert Putnam identifies social capital – the extent of connections within and between social networks – as one of the most important determinants of human happiness in the US;[24] a finding with which Canadian economist and fellow expert in the study of social capital John Helliwell agrees.[25]

But how much do social relationships really matter, then, when they are weighed against other things in our lives?

Using ten years' worth of the British Household Panel Survey (BHPS), the relative importance of three particular social relationship variables upon our well-being can be explored.[26] The first external factor is marriage. The other two related variables consist of how often the survey respondent (i) sees her friends and relatives who live elsewhere; and (ii) talks to her neighbours.

So what is the correlation between money and happiness when (a) personality traits have been all but removed from the happiness equation, and (b) all other observable personal characteristics have been taken into account and are held constant? Imagine that the previous happiness equation now includes observable personal characteristics such as social relationships (marital status, how often the respondents see friends, how often they talk to neighbours), age, education, employment status, where they live, and health – i.e., all the things we could think of that may be correlated with both happiness and income and therefore need to be taken into account in the previously drawn happiness equation – as additional explanatory variables:

$$\text{Happiness}_{i,t} - \overline{\text{Happiness}_i}$$
$$= \beta \times (\text{Income}_{i,t} - \overline{\text{Income}_i})$$
$$+ \delta \times (\text{Personal characteristics}_{i,t} - \overline{\text{Personal characteristics}_i})$$
$$+ (\text{Error term}_{i,t} - \overline{\text{Error term}_i})$$

Similar to the income coefficient, the new symbol δ (delta) represents the estimated correlations between time-demeaned happiness and a whole list of the individual's time-demeaned personal characteristics. Holding the time-demeaned personal characteristics constant, a scatter plot between time-demeaned life-satisfaction[27] scores and time-demeaned income of everyone aged between 16 and 65 in the BHPS produces the best line of fit with a slope (or steepness) of approximately 0.0007. What this means is that a £1,000 increase in income is observed, on average, with a corresponding increase in life satisfaction (or happiness) of 0.0007 (out of 7 life-satisfaction points), holding other things equal.

Newly wedded people report, on average, 0.134 life-satisfaction points higher than when they were singletons. People who start seeing friends and relatives almost every day of the week for a year also report roughly 0.161 life-satisfaction points higher than when they hardly saw their friends and relatives at all. Finally, people who talk to their neighbours almost every day of the week for a year report 0.083 life-satisfaction points higher than when they had no interactions with their neighbours at all.

Now, in order for us to make more sense of these numbers, we can ask how much additional income it would take on average to make (i) a single person be just as satisfied with life as someone who is married; (ii) a person who doesn't see her friends or relatives for a year to be just as satisfied with life as someone who sees her friends almost on a daily basis; and (iii) a person who doesn't talk to her neighbours to be just as satisfied with life as someone who talks to her neighbours almost every day of the week for a year.

So, correcting for the unobserved personality traits bias, in order to compensate someone for being single as opposed to being married, income would have to be [married coefficient/income (in £1,000) coefficient] = 0.134/0.0007 = approximately £200,000 ($300,000) higher, on average, than the current household income. And since we're dealing with a year-to-year change in both income levels and the respondent's marital status, the £200,000 here represents only the value of *the first year* of being married – i.e., the happiness that comes from a one-off move from being single to being married. Still, this is mind-bogglingly large. A slightly larger amount of compensating differential (£230,000 or $345,000) applies for somebody who has no social life whatsoever. Talking to neighbours every day, on the other hand, is worth almost £120,000 ($180,000) in the first year in terms of the happiness that it brings.

These are gigantic amounts. Yet they may have been significantly confounded by the fact that income is endogenous – it's determined by happiness itself, as well as by other things that are directly linked to happiness. (For example, people earning high incomes may work longer hours and spend more time commuting to and from work than others, thus leading to the illusion that income buys little happiness, when in fact it's the lack of a social life that makes a rich person unhappy.)

Correcting for the endogeneity in the income variable – i.e., assuming that money is now serendipitously given to us for 'free' – we arrive at an income coefficient of 0.038 instead of the original 0.0007. In other words, a £1,000 increase in exogenous income is related to a 0.038 increase in the happiness score. This implies that an additional pay rise of 0.134/0.038 = approximately £3,500 ($5,250) is required, on average, to make a single person feel just as happy with life – no more, no less – as if she was recently hitched, holding other things constant. (Note that 0.038 can be thought of as the estimated 'pure' income effect on happiness, i.e., the size of the effect of a windfall on our happiness.) The value is different for social life outside the household; to compensate someone who doesn't see friends or relatives for a year would require an additional income of 0.161/0.038 = approximately £4,000 ($6,000) per annum. To compensate someone who doesn't talk to her neighbours, on the other hand, would require a windfall of £2,100 ($3,150) per annum to be just as satisfied with life as someone who talks to her neighbours every day for a year.

How about children? What is the value of having children for our happiness? While there's no statistical difference in terms of life satisfaction at the cross-section between parents and non-parents – in that parents are no happier with their lives, on average, than non-parents (and we'll come back to this in later chapters) – the first year following the birth of a child is in fact associated with an increase in the respondent's life satisfaction of approximately 0.098 points on a 7-point life satisfaction scale.

And how much is that in terms of money?

Well, for an average person in the UK, the first year of having a child is exactly the same as winning a serendipitous sum of money of around £2,500 ($3,750) for that year.

Or, if you like, the experience of holding your baby son or daughter for the very first time is perhaps no different to the experience of getting a gift basket full of cash.

Pretty shocking, isn't it?

So if social relationships foster happiness, what about separation (or divorce)? Given that a move from being single to being married brings significant joy into our lives, one could also imagine a move from being married to being separated to be associated with a completely opposite emotion. And true to form: while a marriage is worth £3,500 in cash, a separation/divorce is likely to cause an emotional trauma that requires an additional £8,000 ($12,000) in the first year to compensate.

But some words of caution are warranted here. While we may be able to solve the infamous happiness–income relationship problem, our decisions on whether or not to get married, see friends, talk to our neighbours, or even have children are hardly random (or predetermined) – even when our personality traits have been all but accounted for. Instead, they are likely to be influenced partly by the way we may be feeling at the time of making the decision or, worse, by some other omitted time-varying factors such as the kind of neighbourhood we happened to be living in at the time. For this reason, without an appropriate identification strategy in place, it's almost impossible for us to conclude that the causality runs from, say, talking to neighbours to life satisfaction and not the other way round.[28]

Death and disability

While a patch of grey cloud shrouds the true effect of social relationships upon our happiness, the sky is ironically much clearer and the sun shining much more brightly on some of the more negative forces that shape our well-being. For example, unfortunate life events such as the death of loved ones and becoming seriously disabled are typically indiscriminate in nature. What this means is that in most cases they are, holding other things constant, random occurrences. Therefore, it's unlikely that, once their persistent personality traits have been taken into account,[29] there would be a reverse causality that runs from unhappiness to the respondent subsequently experiencing either one of these inauspicious life events. Put another way, their observed correlations with happiness can, in most cases, be considered as readily causal.

For an illustration of how some life events are, by their very nature, randomised while others are not, imagine the decision to have a baby for the first time. Despite the fact that such a decision – especially among married couples – is usually made after careful planning, the sex of the first-born baby in countries where selective abortion by gender is illegal (such as Britain, for example) is completely and utterly randomly assigned by nature. This makes it possible for us to infer that a seemingly unrelated correlation between having a first-born daughter and, say, an increase in each parent's tendency to vote for a left-wing party,[30] or a reduction in such risky health behaviours as smoking, drinking and drug-taking,[31] is causal.

So, how the death of our loved ones and disability are determined is no different to how the sex of your first-born is determined: mostly by chance. If that's the case, then how much would different bereavements be worth in terms of unhappiness? In a study published in the *Journal of Legal Studies*, Andrew Oswald and I estimated a series of mental well-being and life satisfaction equations with deaths as our independent variables of interest.[32] The aim was, of course, to see how much money would need to be given, on average, to compensate someone who has experienced the death of a loved one – especially a child, a spouse or a parent – *without* having to draw upon answers to complex questions about how intensely the person values (or valued) that loved one (simply because such inquiry is difficult and perhaps too morally sensitive to carry out). I mean, can you possibly imagine somebody insensitive enough to ask you how much you value the life of your partner, let alone how much *more* you value the life of your partner *over and above* the life of your child?

And so, at the risk of being forever damned by *Daily Mail* readers, we published the following table in 2008:

Type of death	Compensatory packages
Partner	£312,000
Child	£126,000
Mother	£22,000
Father	£21,000
Friend	£8,000
Sibling	£1,000

Figure 11.

As you can see, on average, the death of a partner – top of the list among the different types of bereavement – requires approximately £312,000 (or $468,000) additional income in the first year to make the person feel just as happy as if she had never experienced such a tragic loss. The loss of a child ranks second in terms of emotional severity at £126,000 (or $189,000) per annum. The death of a mother, father, friend and sibling rank third, fourth, fifth and sixth respectively. Again, these figures are derived simply by dividing each of the death coefficients obtained in the happiness equation by the instrumented (in other words, causal) income coefficient.

The shadow price of becoming severely disabled can also be calculated in the same way. To compensate for serious disability (disability that severely restricts the person from doing day-to-day activities such as dressing or walking up flights of stairs), income would have to be £71,000 ($106,000) higher, on average, than the current household income in the first year[33] – over four times the original one-off financial settlement awarded to the disabled victim in the *West and Son vs. Shephard* case.

Grim statistics

To say that these figures, when they were released to the press for the first time, were frowned upon by the public is a massive understatement. On reading that seeing a friend every day is worth, on average, around £4,000 free money per annum in terms of happiness, a common reaction was disbelief. £4,000 for a friend? A marriage brings the same joy as a £3,500 unexpected pay rise? The death of a child needs only £126,000 in the first year to compensate? What idiot funded this piece of research?[34]

But it's not surprising that many people would find these estimated figures, well, surprising. While there may be some scientific merit to the shadow-pricing method in calculating different types of compensatory damages in court, the implications for other forms of non-marketable goods are less obvious. For example, given that there are no markets for friends or neighbours or children, it seems pointless to know, not whether one experience is better than another but exactly *how much* better. Okay, so these figures may tell us something about what's relatively more important in our lives – for example, seeing friends every day is associated with a bigger hit in terms of happiness compared to having children, *ceteris paribus* – which, of course, would be useful information for some people who may be on the verge of deciding whether or not to have a baby and perhaps leave their social life behind for a few years. But to say that one is worth £1,500 more than the other is absurd. One might even argue that there's no practicality in finding out such information at all.[35]

But imagine this. Imagine that the observed correlation between happiness and the frequency of social interactions with friends tells us something important about the relationship between the way we conduct our social life and our well-being. Imagine also that you have just been offered an optional pay rise of £3,500 in exchange for no social life for a year. Assuming that everything else remains *exactly* the same before and after accepting the pay rise (e.g. hours worked, distance to and from home, your office space, etc.), would you take it?

Based on the above estimated figures, your answer should of course be 'No, sirree!' Here, your reservation wage (the lowest rate at which you would be willing to accept a particular type of job) should be at least an additional £4,000 (i.e. the amount of windfall required as compensation for not seeing a friend for a whole year). But obviously, it's unlikely that such a scenario will exist in real life: it's hard to imagine why any company would be willing to pay their employees £4,000 on top of their current salary in exchange for such a ridiculous thing in return. More realistic, however, is that a job offer will come with a pay package £4,000 higher than your old job, but that you will be expected to take a lot more responsibility by working extremely long hours in a much more stressful environment, while at the same time spending a lot of your time commuting – all of which will inevitably result in you having no social life at all for a year. Now, would you take it?

Well, not unless the per-annum pay rise for that year is at least £230,000 and not £4,000 as in the previous case (the £230,000, of course, being the shadow price of friendship when income is not serendipitously or exogenously given to us). The reason is that the proposed pay rise of £230,000 isn't given in exchange for just the lack of social life you are going to have to endure from taking up the job. You not having a social life is merely one of the outcomes (rather than the *only* outcome), a collateral damage from having an extremely stressful job. The ridiculous sum of money, in this case, is conditioned on you having to sacrifice not only an active social life, but perhaps also your own day-to-day mental well-being from having to work too hard, seven days a week.

In other words, the £230,000 reflects the other changes that could be brought about from accepting a stressful job (other factors that are correlated with both social relationships and happiness) but are nevertheless *not* held constant in the happiness equation.

But the interesting question is: how many of us would actually be willing to accept a job with a pay rise of a lot less than £230,000 in exchange for our own peace of mind and well-being?

Well, sadly, just about everyone I know, I think. Myself included, probably.

CHAPTER 6

DOES TIME REALLY HEAL ALL WOUNDS?

So, perhaps unsurprisingly, one of the main messages we can gather from the previous chapter is that the death of loved ones and disability hurt. And judging by how much extra money over and above our current income is required, on average, to compensate us for the onset of each of these heartbreaking circumstances – for example, £312,000 for the death of a partner – both seem to hurt like hell. Yet what we don't precisely know is exactly how long it's going to hurt like hell for. Three years? Five years? A lifetime?

Surely not. Surely losing somebody we love or losing our physical ability to function normally can't hurt like hell for the rest of our lives.

After all, if the old saying is true, then time will heal all wounds, right?

Before we go any further, let's imagine for a second that – contrary to the conventional wisdom that time heals all wounds – time really doesn't have the ability to fix our broken hearts at all, no matter how long we wait. If this is the case, then imagine the kind of ethical and practical implications for tort cases of wrongful death, where compensatory damages are awarded by judges to the victims as a lump-sum, one-off payment rather than repeatedly for every year thereafter.

Would the one-off payment system still seem fair? If the death of someone you love hurts you like a fresh wound every day for the rest of your life, then shouldn't you also be compensated for that mind-numbing pain every day of your life too?

Set-point theory

Philip Brickman's parents knew early on that their son was gifted with something very special, that he saw the world in ways not many others could. Born in 1943 in Montreal, Canada, his extraordinary mental abilities were already apparent as a child; he was reading well before he was three, and was promoted from grade two to four because he was so far ahead of his peers. He also made valedictorian of his high school class, a privilege given to only one person in each graduating year.

Brickman went on to earn his Bachelor's degree from Harvard University, where he graduated *magna cum laude* in 1964. He then went on to discover his passion for psychology at Michigan State University, where he received his Ph.D. in 1968. Believing that social psychology should be a field that deals with fundamental human concerns, he began his academic career investigating important humane topics such as commitment and caring, coping, persistence and, of course, happiness.

In collaboration with his close colleagues Dan Coates and Ronnie Janoff-Bulman, Philip Brickman produced one of the most widely known studies about human happiness to date, published in the *Journal of Personality and Social Psychology* in 1978. The three psychologists set out their research strategy by asking an important, yet relatively simple question about our subjective well-being: Is happiness relative?[1] Comparing 22 lottery winners with 22 controls, and a group of 29 paralysed accident victims who had been interviewed previously, they found that lottery winners were no happier than people in the control group. In fact, they even took significantly less pleasure from a series of mundane events compared to the controls. But what's perhaps even more surprising is that they found only small differences in self-reported happiness levels between the controls and the paraplegics.

Put another way, the paraplegics were, controversially, only slightly less happy than the lottery winners.

Such an apparent divide between what we expect these people's happiness levels to be (*the lottery winners should be a lot happier than the controls, while the controls should be a lot happier than the paraplegics*) and what the data actually say, led Philip and his colleagues to conclude that human beings a) adapt to tragic life events, such as disability and the death of loved ones; and b) habituate to positive experiences, such as lottery wins.

And based on such small differences in happiness levels between these three groups of lottery winners, controls and accident victims, many have even interpreted Brickman and his colleagues' findings of adaptation and habituation as a complete, full-on phenomenon: that time not only *completely* heals all wounds, but also effectively dampens the 'ups' of any positive experiences that we may encounter in our lifetime.

Despite the fact that the cross-sectional data set (observations of different people at one point of time) used by Brickman was extremely tiny (22 lottery winners, 22 controls, and 29 accident victims), the impact of the study on the field of psychology was huge. Soon after its publication in 1978, many psychologists began discussing the possibility that human beings may be endowed with happiness 'set points' in that people initially react to events, but then return to baseline factors determined by personality traits;[2] hence the so-called 'set-point' theory. And according to this theory, all humans have considerable ability to bounce back from any negative shocks in life in a reasonably short period of time.

This is a huge claim, even for psychologists, and it definitely made the three pioneering researchers – especially Philip Brickman – very proud. But sadly, before the set-point theory had a chance to advance further, Philip's life ended tragically on 13 May 1982, just four years after his famous publication, when he took his own life at the age of 38.

The news of Philip Brickman's suicide came like a thunderbolt to his fellow psychologists. How could somebody considered by those close to him as a devoted father, a family man, and a beloved colleague and friend decide to end his own life when he had just about everything going for him? To many, his death also raised a puzzling question: If time heals all wounds, and he of all people knows that it does, why did he do what he did? Why did he not let time do the work that he knew for certain it would?

In his obituary,[3] his close friends and colleagues, the psychologists Camille Wortman and Dan Coates, made a touching observation from Brickman's studies on happiness: that, although time may heal all wounds, positive emotion itself is also fleeting and temporary, and we need never-ending gratification in order to 'just' stay as content as we were. They also wrote:

> We cannot rely on others to provide much consolation when yesterday's thrill becomes tomorrow's tedium. [And] the best way off the hedonic treadmill, according to Phil's writings, is commitment – the almost magical mechanism that converts the inevitable pain and dissatisfaction in life into purpose and meaningfulness. Unfortunately, commitments can be very fragile, in part because they are based on such irrational mechanisms. [Phil's] writings reveal deep feelings for the phenomena he studied; perhaps he had too much feeling and too much insight. These two things together are the mainsprings of unique creative achievement, but they are also the elements of tragedy.

And so, as Wortman and Coates believed, the idea that human beings are bounded to only one happiness set point, shaped long ago by our inborn personality traits, may have played a vital role in their friend's suicide. While good for tragedies, the set-point theory also implies that, because of the habituation effect, there's virtually nothing in our lives that can possibly have a long-lasting impact upon our happiness. In order to stay happy, hard work and commitment are required. But, knowing that whatever we do will have only a fleeting impact upon our happiness, how many of us can actually stay committed to making ourselves happy for a lifetime?

A scientifically unattractive division

Following Brickman's death, there have been many writings in psychology providing evidential support for his seminal idea that happiness and unhappiness are merely transitory reactions to people's change in circumstances, and that any efforts to strive for long-run happiness are futile. For a start, many psychologists have found that for external life circumstances – such as money,[4] objective health[5] and even beauty[6] – though they have noticeable relationships with happiness, the size of their correlation (making up around 20 per cent of the variance in happiness) pales in comparison against measures of personality traits (making up 80 per cent, or the rest of the variance).[7] Other cross-sectional studies have also reported complementary findings to Brickman's lottery and paraplegic results. For instance, there's evidence of blind people reporting almost the same level of happiness, on average, as those with perfect sight,[8] and there's insignificant difference in self-reported well-being between haemodialysis patients and healthy non-patients.[9] And so a consensus was made within psychology that Philip

Brickman was most likely right all along about the ephemeral nature of our emotions.

Nothing in life – good or bad – seems to last for ever. Well, at least in terms of happiness, anyway.

But wait a minute. What have psychologists' close cousins – the conventional economists – got to say about the set-point theory?

'Complete nonsense!' would probably be one of their predictable replies. Unlike assumptions normally used in the psychological literature, standard economics textbooks assume a given utility (or happiness) function in which there is generically no habituation or adaptation.[10]

In other words, if the death of our loved one hurts like hell in the first year, economists say that it will hurt like hell – in exactly equal measure – for as long as we live, which seems wholly unrealistic.

But why is that? Why didn't conventional economists just listen to the evidence provided by Philip Brickman and his fellow psychologists all those years ago and use it to construct a better utility model that allows for both habituation and adaptation as additional features? Perhaps it's a pride thing. Or maybe it's because conventional economists believe that psychologists' findings on habituation and adaptation are wrong.

For a start, many economists believe that the sample sizes often used in these psychological studies are way too small (remember that the sample used in Brickman et al's study contained only between 20 and 30 people in each of the three groups). With tiny sample sizes (those with fewer than 100 observations overall), we risk running into a Type II error. In statistics, a Type II error is an error associated with the failure to observe a difference when in truth there is one (an example would be a test of a small group of smokers and non-smokers showing that, on average, there's no statistically significant association between smoking and lung cancer, when in fact there is one). With only a few tens of people represented in each group, it's difficult to tell whether the almost zero differences in happiness levels between lottery winners, paraplegics and control subjects are due to habituation or adaptation, or simply because we haven't cast a wide enough net to cover more people and make the results representative across all groups.

Yet another issue that economists have with Brickman's study and many other subsequent studies on habituation and adaptation in psychology is that their interpretations are based largely on patterns observed at the cross-section – comparing different people's happiness at the same point of time. And the trouble with this method is that most cross-sectional patterns are only suggestive rather than causal, especially when we want to test for hedonic adaptation and habituation effects to many events in our lives. The famous Brickman study, though it managed to spark serious discussions about the nature of human happiness among social scientists, is nevertheless scientifically flawed.

To explain this, it's important to understand why the Brickman study is controversial in the first place. It's controversial because its results are deeply counter-intuitive. One would expect, of course, lottery winners to be extremely happy and paraplegics to be extremely miserable with their lives – but surprisingly these aren't reflected in the data set. So, it's possible that the cross-sectional patterns may not signify habituation or adaptation at all. Rather, they may merely reflect the fact that all of us, including Brickman and co., tend to overestimate precisely *how much* lottery wins and disability affect our happiness, leading to the conclusion that the results – that there are few differences in well-being between these three groups – are surprising when in fact they are not.

Many of these psychological studies are not comparing like with like, which is essentially what needs to be done. Because people's personality traits are often not taken into account in cross-sectional studies for the obvious reason that they are not readily observable in normal surveys, a reasonable conjecture from Brickman's results would be that people with sunny dispositions may engage in more risky behaviours than others (and therefore are more accident-prone and hence more likely to end up paralysed), while at the same time reporting unusually high levels of happiness. As for those who are less extraverted – those who don't enjoy the company of others – they may tend to buy more lottery tickets, and have a higher chance of winning than others, while at the same time reporting unusually low levels of happiness.

What we effectively need to do – in order to tease out whether or not hedonic adaptation and habituation are 'real' phenomena – is to track the reported happiness of the same individuals longitudinally (for a long period of time) before and after the life experience in question.

Anything less than that and we'll have a hard time convincing any social scientists, let alone economists, that time really heals all wounds.

A good partnership

There's possibly no tougher person to be measured up against in the world of psychology than Ed Diener. A professor at the University of Illinois and one of the world's leading experts on happiness and positive psychology, 'Dr Happy' has written more than 200 academic papers on human emotions. His devotion to the subject is also second to none, and it even has a spill-over effect on his son's interests. Prior to 2005, the psychologist Robert Biswas-Diener, also known as 'the Indiana Jones of Positive Psychology', spent several years travelling the globe collecting happiness data from, among others, the African Maasai, the Greenland Inughuit, the Amish, and the slum-dwellers of Calcutta.[11] Together, Robert and his dad wrote a paper about how people are generally happy with their lives no matter where they are in the world.

Around the same time, over 4,000 miles away across the pond, English economist Andrew Clark of the Paris School of Economics was working on a topic in happiness to which many economists didn't even give a second thought: is there a psychological scar from unemployment? Put another way, are we bound to be less happy the greater has been our experience of unemployment in the past? In a paper published in *Economica* in 2001 with economists Yannis Georgellis of Brunel University and Peter Sanfey of the University of Kent, the three scholars were able to show, using a time-demeaned (so personality traits were completely removed from the analysis) nationally-representative longitudinal data set from Germany, that the unemployed are significantly less satisfied with their lives compared to those in full-time employment. And yet unemployment hurts less psychologically the longer the person has been unemployed in the past.[12] More particularly, they were able to show that, holding other things like income and age constant, an unemployed man who has been jobless for approximately 60 per cent of his active months in the labour market over the past three years is indifferent between employment and unemployment (although we don't know if it was continuous unemployment for 60 per cent of this period). And there's more to it than that. What the three economists didn't realise at the time was that their work was probably the first nationally-representative, longitudinal evidence of adaptation to a change in our experiences.

Not bad for a year's work on an important psychological theory done by economists.

While Ed Diener and Andrew Clark have achieved considerable respect from each side of the academic stratosphere, psychology for Ed and economics for Andrew, both knew that more could be done to either accept or reject Philip Brickman's claim of complete adaptation to different life experiences. And both knew they needed the other's help to succeed.

So, at the beginning of the new millennium, the prominent psychologist Ed Diener, along with his former Ph.D. student Richard Lucas, decided to join force with economists Andrew Clark and Yannis Georgellis to study whether happiness really has the ability to adapt and habituate to just about anything that life brings us.

The things that hurt and the time that heals

The first life experience to be studied in detail by the four scholars was unemployment, which wasn't surprising considering that half the people conducting the research were economists.[13] But instead of comparing the happiness of the unemployed relative to the employed, the researchers took one bold step further and tracked only the life satisfaction of those individuals who would eventually become unemployed, one year before it happened and then in the years that followed while they *continued* to remain in unemployment.

It wouldn't take a genius to predict that unemployment lowers happiness. One reason for this is obvious: the lack of a constant stream of income from being unemployed can be unappealing to many individuals. But it has also been found repeatedly that the unemployed continue to report substantially lower levels of happiness relative to the employed with exactly the *same* household incomes – perhaps due to social stigma and the loss of self-esteem.[14]

So, psychologically, unemployment seems to hurt *per se*.

And that seems to be what the two psychologists and the two economists (or the *psychonomists* hereafter) uncovered with the German longitudinal data set. There is a substantial and abrupt drop in life satisfaction at the first year of the person becoming unemployed, i.e., at year = 0 in Figure 12. But there's something else too. It appears that unemployment doesn't feel as bad after a couple of years into unemployment. So Philip Brickman may have been right all along about the existence of happiness set points, and that adaptation is a real phenomenon.

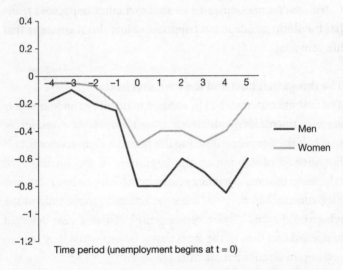

Figure 12. The dynamic effect of unemployment on life satisfaction. Unemployment begins at time = 0 and continues through to time = 5.

But that's not the end of it. Contrary to the set-point theory stating that people react to events but then return to baseline levels of happiness and satisfaction over time, what the psychonomists also found is that while human beings indeed bounce back from unemployment, the adaptation is *far from complete* even after more than five years spent without work, especially for men, for whom unemployment continues to hurt psychologically throughout. And so, even though life seems to improve significantly for the jobless only a few years into unemployment, it will never be as good as it used to be before unemployment, according to the psychonomists, no matter how long it takes.

That's half a point each to psychologists who believe in complete adaptation to events and to economists who don't believe in adaptation at all.

But maybe unemployment is just a one-off case? Maybe we're able to adapt much better to other life circumstances than we can to unemployment? In an article published in the highly-regarded *Economic Journal* in 2008, the psychonomists built upon their earlier work on unemployment and, using the same German longitudinal data set, examined not only whether there's adaptation or habituation to different life circumstances, but also whether people anticipate these life circumstances taking place well in advance.[15]

Do we, in other words, react to some life events that haven't happened yet but that will categorically occur some time in the future?

Definitely.

Take separation and divorce, for example. It's widely known that, at the cross-section, separated and divorced people are significantly less happy with their lives compared to their married counterparts. However, the psychonomists provided evidence that, on average, people's satisfaction with life in fact declines slowly but steadily for up to four years for men and two years for women before the divorce.[16] Adaptation to the breakdown in marriage that occurs just a year afterwards is, however, rapid and complete. Life satisfaction is even higher four years into the separation and divorce than it was during marriage.

So, couples who have been experiencing a decline in life satisfaction – perhaps through worsening marital conditions – are more likely to be separated or get a divorce, which isn't at all surprising. What's more surprising is that these separated individuals and divorcees seem to be getting over it a lot quicker than one might have predicted.

And how long does it take on average to get over the pain of divorce?

Two years for men, and three for women.

So perhaps John Kenneth Galbraith, one of the most famous economists, was right all along when he said: 'The happiest time in any man's life is just after the first divorce.'

What about the death of our loved ones? Our intuition, of course, tells us that, unlike divorce, it's almost impossible for anyone to react emotionally to a death that hasn't happened yet, and that if there's one thing we can never get over, no matter how long it takes, it's the death of someone we love.

Well, our intuition is at least right about one thing: according to the psychonomists, there seems to be no substantial evidence of a significant anticipation effect to the future death of our wife or husband (there is indeed a drop of well-being one year prior to widowhood, but an extremely small one). The pattern appears to suggest that we don't become significantly unhappy before becoming a widow or a widower. Death is, as anticipated, more of a random occurrence than a predetermined incidence.

But just when we thought that time would never heal this piercing wound, it does. And it only takes, on average, a little over two years for widowers and four years for widows to bounce back completely from the death of their partner – at least, in terms of their life satisfaction (see Figure 13).

The main conclusion is grossly perplexing. How can it take what seems like for ever to completely adapt to unemployment,

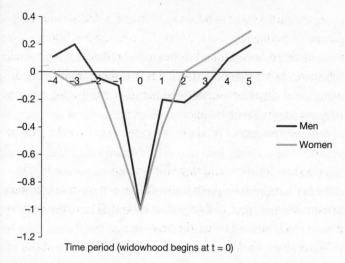

Figure 13. The dynamic effect of widowhood on life satisfaction; widowhood begins at time = 0.

but only a few years to get over the death of loved ones? Surely, the so-called psychonomists have to be wrong about this?

Well, not if the same patterns can be repeated for other nationally-representative longitudinal data sets. Consistency is a prerequisite for the psychonomists' findings to be convincing beyond reasonable doubt.

At the end of the summer in 2005, Andrew Oswald and I decided to conduct a test of whether or not British people recover as quickly – psychologically – from the death of loved ones as the sample in the German data set.[17] They do. It takes roughly one year to adapt (almost) completely to the significant distress that the death of a husband, a wife or a child brings us. In a separate study, Andrew Oswald and Jonathan Gardner discovered that people also have an incredible ability to adapt completely and quickly to a painful divorce (less than two years on average).[18] Unemployment, by contrast, takes a much longer time, if not for ever, to adapt to.[19] And when we do, it's only partial. Incomplete.

And what's more, in a recent study by Paul Frijters, David Johnston and Michael Shields, the three economists found using an Australian longitudinal data set that people tend to adapt quickly to both death of spouses and separation, but not to unemployment.[20]

All of these results lead to one contentious conclusion: what the psychonomists found was not a stand-alone result. Three different nationally-representative longitudinal data sets have helped confirm this. We adapt much quicker to the pain of divorce and, incredibly, to the death of our loved ones than to the pain of unemployment.

How bizarre.

And what about some of the things many of us believe we could *definitely* get used to with time? Things like time spent commuting to and from work, which many of us do *by choice*? Surely, if we can adapt quickly and fully to the death of loved ones, adapting to what can only be described as 'a relatively mild unpleasant experience' should be a walk in the park for us?

Well, you'd be surprised.

According to two Swiss economists and happiness experts, Bruno Frey of the University of Zurich and Alois Stutzer of the University of Basel, time spent commuting to and from work is like time spent with the devil. Using longitudinal data for Germany, the two scholars found that time spent commuting has a clear and noticeable psychic cost – perhaps due to stress and the loss of valuable time that could be spent elsewhere more meaningfully – which can be compensated for only by a substantial pay rise; they found that people who commute 23 minutes (one way), which is the average commuting time in

Germany, would have to earn 19 percentage points more each month, on average, to be fully compensated.[21]

But what makes it worse is that, over time, they found *no adaptation whatsoever* to the stress and unpleasantness brought about by time spent commuting. Commuters start unhappy and stay equally unhappy throughout the years of having to do the commute.

Why is that? How could time possibly heal the deep wounds of bereavement and divorce fully and quickly, but do only a slow and half-hearted job on the inconveniences of unemployment and commuting? First, let's ask the following question. If time doesn't completely heal all wounds, what about the good times? How long do different good times last?

Habituation to good feelings

The best personal account I've read on the subject of habituation doesn't actually come from one of the fellow academics I admire – not Ed Diener, Richard Easterlin, Daniel Gilbert or even Andrew Oswald – but from Andre Agassi, the former world number one tennis player and, so far, one of only two winners of the Golden Slam (Australian Open, French Open, Wimbledon, US Open, and Olympic Gold).[22] After winning Wimbledon in 1992, he summed up, in his critically-acclaimed memoir, almost everything we need to know about our happiness:

> Now that I've won [Wimbledon], I know something that very few people on earth are permitted to know. A win doesn't feel as good as a loss feels bad, and the good feeling doesn't last as long as the bad. Not even close.[23]

What makes Andre Agassi's experience so interesting is that he's right – not many people have achieved what he has achieved.

And for that reason, we can only imagine what it must have felt like to be him in that summer of 1992, to live the dream like Andre. So we tell ourselves it should have been one of the best experiences in the world. It should even have felt better than winning the lottery, because he could tell himself afterwards that he earned it; he deserved to feel happy about such a tremendous achievement. It should also have made up for any losses he had ever had to face along the way to becoming Wimbledon champion. We believe the good feelings that come from winning a Wimbledon title will last for ever; a new and permanently higher happiness set point.

Yet, as we can see from Andre's account of his experience, that's not the case. But why didn't the win make up for all the losses beforehand? And why didn't he stay extremely happy for very long after winning Wimbledon?

First, Agassi's comment, 'A win doesn't feel as good as a loss feels bad', is a perfect description of a human behaviour that psychologists Amos Tversky and Daniel Kahneman called 'loss aversion'.[24] Loss aversion, in simple terms, describes our strong tendency to prefer avoiding losses to actually acquiring gains. In other words, there's a clear asymmetry here between the effects of wins and losses on our happiness.

We love to win. But we hate losing even more.

Tversky and Kahneman illustrated this point by asking a group of randomly selected individuals a simple experimental question. Consider this for a minute:

Imagine that as part of your professional training you were assigned to a part-time job. The training is now ending and you must look for employment. You consider two possibilities. They are like your training job in most respects except for the amount of social contact and the convenience of commuting to and from work. To compare the two jobs to each other and to the present one you have made up the following table:

Job	Contact with others	Commute time
Present job	Isolated for long stretches	10 minutes
Job A	Limited contact with others	20 minutes
Job D	Moderately sociable	60 minutes

Which job would you choose? Job A or Job D?[25]

According to the two eminent psychologists, around 70 per cent of participants prefer Job A to Job D; the majority seem to prefer spending ten more minutes commuting and having a slightly more social life than spending 50 more minutes commuting and having a moderately sociable lifestyle.

However, the same people are then presented with the same options, but with the reference (or the present job) changed:

Job	Contact with others	Commute time
Present job	Much pleasant social interaction	80 minutes
Job A	Limited contact with others	20 minutes
Job D	Moderately sociable	60 minutes

Surprisingly, only 33 per cent prefer Job A to Job D. More people now seem to prefer a trade-off between less commuting time and a small reduction in social interaction to a trade-off between much less commuting time and a large fall in their social life.

What Tversky and Kahneman were implying is that, in general, a given difference between two options will have greater impact if it's viewed as a difference between two disadvantages than if it's viewed as a difference between two advantages. And for this reason, people tend to be more sensitive to the dimension in which they are losing relative to the reference point, thus leading to 70 per cent of the people choosing Job *A* in the first scenario as opposed to 33 per cent in the second scenario.

Such asymmetry between how we view gains and losses is puzzling, but it helps explain why a win doesn't feel as good as a loss feels bad, why a windfall of £100 may not yield happiness that is the same as the unhappiness brought about by a loss of £100, or even why a marriage will not make us as happy as a break-up will make us unhappy (recalling from our previous chapter that a marriage is worth £3,500 in cash, while a separation/divorce requires up to £8,000 to compensate in the first year).

But what about Agassi's comment that the 'good feeling doesn't last as long as the bad'? Is that a true description of how we normally adapt to positive experiences as well?

Unfortunately, much as we would like to conduct a study on how long it takes to adapt to the elation of becoming a Wimbledon champion, we don't have the means or resources to do so. Thankfully, there are many other positive experiences that have been studied in detail, one of which is an increase in income.

We know from previous chapters that income does buy happiness (albeit not as much as one might think). What is less known, however, is how long it takes for an average person to adapt to a rise in his or her income. Three happiness experts, economist Robert MacCulloch of Imperial College London, John Haisken-DeNew from Germany, and former fencing Olympian from Argentina and now business professor at Harvard Business School, Rafael Di Tella, made an attempt to figure this one out.[26] Again, using the now familiar German longitudinal data set, the three scholars found that it takes us merely four years to completely habituate to a 50 per cent increase in our household income. There is, though, less habituation to a positive psychological effect from moving up in the social status ranking – i.e., I become happy and remain happy over time if I manage to move up the social ranking order by, for example, getting a more prestigious occupation than my peers. This is, of course, consistent with the Easterlin Paradox (see Chapter 3), which states that an increase in income over time doesn't lead to an increase in the aggregate happiness for the population, but when we take a snapshot of a country we are more likely to see that relatively higher-status individuals are generally much happier than people of lower status.

Okay, money buys happiness, but only fleetingly. That's hardly surprising, considering that it doesn't buy a lot of happiness for us in the first place. But how about something else that we know would give us a big hit in our psychological well-being? How about the joy we get from marriage, for instance?

Well, according to the psychonomists, there is indeed strong evidence that people tend to become significantly happier with their lives in the years leading up to their marriage. The positive effect of marriage peaks, as one would expect, at the year of marriage itself. But how long does this so-called 'honeymoon period' last? Five years? Ten years? Till death do us part?

Two years. *Two years*? Yes, that's how long it takes, on average, to get completely used to the initial joy brought about by marriage (see Figure 14). That's even quicker than our ability to habituate to a rise in income.[27]

What about the happiness from having children? Surely there should be no way we will be able to habituate to that?

Not quite, I'm afraid. The truth is that it doesn't even last for more than a year afterwards. People generally become happier

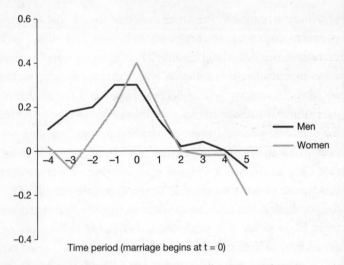

Figure 14. The dynamic effect of marriage on life satisfaction; marriage begins at time = 0 and continues through to time = 5.

with life just a few years before having a child, and this happiness peaks at the year of the child's birth. However, the positive effect of having children seems to disappear completely – even turns into a negative effect – in the first year after he or she is born. And we only 'just' adapt to the lowered happiness when the child turns five years old.

Needless to say, these are controversial and disturbing results. Yet, like the evidence on negative experiences, they aren't what you'd call a rarity. For instance, the findings that parents aren't always significantly happier than non-parents are hardly new. There's overwhelming evidence from all over the world suggesting that while the birth of a child is associated with a positive hit on our happiness, life satisfaction, marital satisfaction and day-to-day mental well-being in general, the same can't be said about the impact of having children in the years that follow.[28]

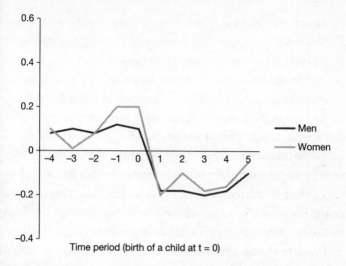

Figure 15. The dynamic effect of the birth of a child on life satisfaction; birth of a child at time = 0.

So, generally speaking, Andre Agassi is right. A win doesn't feel as good as a loss feels bad, and we tend to habituate much more fully to positive feelings than we adapt to bad ones. And for some of the bad experiences in our lives such as unemployment and long commutes, time doesn't seem to have the ability to completely heal the wounds. But can there be some positive experiences – other than increase in status – that we don't habituate to?

Now that I have your attention

The answers, of course, lie within the explanations of how we adapt and habituate psychologically in the first place. This is a job for theorists.

First up is a Nobel laureate in economics, Gary Becker of Chicago University, and his young colleague, economist Luis Rayo. In their seminal study published in the *Journal of*

Political Economy, Becker and Rayo propose that happiness was shaped long ago by natural selection.[29] The key motivation of their study is the idea that, through evolution, there is a natural upper and lower bound on the levels of happiness that can be experienced by the individual. Because of natural selection, we are really the best version of ourselves, since the genes of those who couldn't adapt to the changing environment didn't get passed on. And so, like blood pressure, where there exists a healthy upper and lower bound, happiness also has a healthy range. And if our happiness can fall within that range, we are assumed to have the motivation we need to go through our lives and pass on our genes as efficiently as possible.

In other words, like the ability of the human eye to adjust quickly to changes in the amount of light, Becker and Rayo argue that nature might have done the same with human happiness by optimally designing it to behave in exactly the same way.

But according to Andrew Oswald and Liam Graham, an economist at University College London, our ability to adapt to bad experiences might be due to something entirely different. The two economists propose that happiness isn't just a flow, which is how we normally think about the nature of happiness, but also a stock of pleasant feelings that can be stored for a reasonable period of time. Central to the concept that they call 'hedonic capital' is the notion that we are programmed to stock up some of this happiness over time, which can then be used on rainy days in order to smooth out any bad shocks in our lives.[30]

The two economic theories make plausible sense. Yet given that we are, after all, talking about happiness, it seems virtually impossible to ignore what psychologists have to say about the processes behind why we adapt and habituate. And who could do a better job at explaining this than the famous double-act of Dan Gilbert and Timothy Wilson?

In 2008, the author of the *New York Times* bestseller *Stumbling on Happiness*, Harvard psychologist Dan Gilbert, and the author of the critically-acclaimed *Strangers to Ourselves*, psychology professor Timothy Wilson of the University of Virginia, published a paper describing the process whereby happiness responses to emotional events – both good and bad – weaken after one or more exposures.[31] And here's how.

First, whenever we come across a novel life event – like having a child for the first time or experiencing the death of our partner – the first thing that's likely to pop into our head is: 'How does this make me happy or unhappy?' Gilbert and Wilson called this process the *attending* period. If the event in question is novel, one that we haven't encountered before, it's likely to attract most of our thoughts and attention as soon as it occurs (and sometimes before it occurs, as in the case of marriage). Consequently, we begin screening out information that's unrelated to our processing goals.

The second process is *reacting* to that particular emotional event. If the event in question has been registered in our brain to be important to our goals, motives or concerns, it's likely to elicit a strong emotional response from us, especially if it's poorly understood. In cases where the event is novel but nevertheless perfectly understood – the death of a loved one from a long-term illness would be a common example here – our emotional responses are unlikely to be as intense as if the event is novel and unexplained.

Once we have encountered such experiences, the third process on their list is us *explaining* the phenomenon to ourselves. What happens here is that we try to assign a meaning to an unexplained event that has recently had an impact on our lives. Why did it happen? Did I deserve to win the lottery? Why did I get married to this girl? What explains this bad grade I just got for my mid-term exams?

In a word, rationalisation occurs. After we have reacted to an event, what happens next is that we begin to rationalise why the event happened to us in the first place. Provided that we succeed in our attempt at explaining the event – and when I say explain, I mean that we are able to find out what the event is, why it occurred, how it fits into what makes us who we are, and what it means more broadly – we will then arrive at the fourth and final process, which is the *adaptation* itself. Once an event is perfectly understood, perhaps after a long exposure to it, we will then adapt or habituate to the event inasmuch as we attend less to it, thus leading to smaller emotional reactions to it. Gilbert and Wilson called these four steps towards affective adaptation AREA (Attend, React, Explain, and Adapt).

Because happiness is essentially a state of mind, Gilbert and Wilson's psychological model AREA seems to make the most sense out of the three models proposed above. Nature might have designed us this way, but it's what goes on in our brain that determines how fast and how fully we adapt to what life has thrown at us. But can it also be used to explain the strange results discussed earlier in this chapter? For example, why we tend to adapt relatively rapidly and fully to the death of loved ones and divorce but not to unemployment and commuting? And why we get used to the joy of having more money, being married, and having children so surprisingly quickly?

Well, we can only hypothesise, of course.

The key word here is *attention*. According to Gilbert and Wilson, we are beginning to adapt to an event if – and perhaps only if – our attention has withered away from it. That is, once an event is better explained to us, we begin to think less and less about it. And when we do think about it, our affective reaction will be relatively weak because the event is already well understood. However, if the event in question requires attending to all the time like a constant reminder, provided that it's well explained, our emotional response to it will be weaker but it will never go away completely.

Time, it seems, completely heals only the wounds that don't constantly require our attention.

And so, one conjecture might be that we tend to spend a lot of time thinking about the death of our loved one within the first year of it occurring. It tears us apart. We believe that the pain will never go away. But in many ways the death of someone we love is also often shared by others, many of whom are also the people we love. We turn to each other for support by encouraging each other to think only about the good in the person who has passed. This is further supported by the funeral and the memorial service, both of which help us to think of death in a different light. We are here to celebrate his or her life, many clergymen and women would say at the beginning of a funeral. Sooner or later, we begin rationalising as well as realising that death is a normal part of life. We accept it, and move on. And whenever we think about our loved one in the years that follow, we tend not to think about their death any more but rather the way they lived their life. And the outcome? A fast and complete adaptation to the death of our loved one occurs.

It should then come as no surprise to learn why we tend to adapt fully and quickly to a divorce. Once it takes place, the pain is there. But we also know well in advance the reasons why we are getting the divorce. As many data sets suggest, we are increasingly unhappy as part of a married couple. Here, the event is more or less already well understood before it even takes place. And so, like the death of our loved one, it probably won't take a lot of time for us to adapt fully to the pain of separation.

But what about unemployment, and the time it takes for us to get to and from work every day? What explains why there's little adaptation to these events? Again, attention plays a key role here. For unemployment, it's fair to say that even though there's some evidence showing unemployment to hurt less psychologically the longer the person has been unemployed in the past, the adaptation process is *far from complete*. This is partly because the unemployed person will continue to think about his status every day, regardless of how long he has been without a job. This is simply because, well, there's nothing else but unemployment for him to think about. I have very little money. I have nothing else to do. I can't get another job. Why is this happening to me? Other people seem to have a job, why not me? These constant streams of thought are likely to be salient, tugging and pulling, for as long as the person remains in unemployment. Similarly with commute time, because time spent commuting is exactly the kind of experience that requires attending to while we're experiencing it. I hate spending two hours on the tube every day. Why is it so crowded in here? This train smells funny. I think I'm going to be sick. The emotional impact is unlikely to change much over time for as long as we continue to commute. And the outcome? You guessed it. There will be little adaptation occurring over time for these events.[32]

Turning to the rate of habituation to good experiences like a pay rise, marriage, and having a baby, the AREA model predicts that we will think about these events a lot within the first year of them occurring. However, if we ask ourselves this question: How many minutes of the day do we spend thinking about how much money we now have in our bank account after the pay rise, or how good it is to be married, or how wonderful it is to have a baby, *three years* into it? My best guess would be: not a lot. The reason for this is simple. It's because, unlike unemployment and time spent commuting, these positive events aren't the kind of experiences that require a lot of attending to afterwards, unless, of course, we're prompted to think about them.

But having a baby is different, you might argue. Having and raising a baby requires a lot of attending to, a lot of care and attention, and surely our happiness should last us a lifetime? How come it doesn't match with what the data are telling us?

Not to worry. I'll be devoting the whole of Chapter 8 to discussing exactly why that's the case, why there's such a difference between what intuitions tell us and what the data sets are telling us. But first, even if there is at last a sign that economists (who believe in no adaptation) and psychologists (who believe in complete adaptation) can converge in their thinking, there's still one unanswered question, a question that many economists love to ask: So what?

So what if we adapt to bad shocks? So what if we habituate to good things in our lives? *So what*? Why should we even care about it if it's within our nature to adapt and habituate and there's nothing we can do to change it?

Think back to the beginning of this book when we were discussing the best way to compensate families in court for the wrongful death of someone they loved. Given the overwhelming evidence suggesting that the death of our loved ones will not continue to hurt like hell for ever, the current system whereby the judge awards a one-off, lump-sum payment to the plaintiff may be considered justifiable. However, in cases where the unfortunate event is of the kind that time can't fully heal, then it seems important for the judge to take this into account when trying to work out how much money should be awarded to the plaintiff. Take severe disability, for example. In 2008, Andrew Oswald and I published a study in the *Journal of Public Economics* describing how adaptation to severe disability is only 30 per cent complete even after more than five years spent being disabled – perhaps because the severely disabled continue to think morbidly about their conditions every day, even as time passes.[33] Then it seems important – even a duty – for judges to make an adjustment for the way the person's happiness may not rebound completely.

For example, let's recall from the previous chapter that the amount of money required to compensate an average person with a serious disability is approximately £71,000 in the first year. Assuming that over five years human beings adapt, on average, to up to 30 per cent of the initial drop in happiness caused by the onset of a serious disability, then the amount of money required to compensate a seriously disabled person in the fifth year of being disabled will be approximately £71,000 × (100 per cent of happiness – 30 per cent drop in happiness) = £50,000 (or 70 per cent of £71,000). If we assume a constant compensation time-path from the first year through to the fifth year, then the compensation package will be £71,000 in the first year of becoming seriously disabled; £65,750 in the second year; £60,500 in the third year; £55,250 in the fourth year; and £50,000 in the fifth year.

In addition to such practical applications, provided that we're well equipped with knowledge of the AREA model, it may also be possible for us to choose not only the kind of experiences that will give the biggest hit in terms of our happiness, but also the kind of hit that lasts. It's true that, apart from status, less is known about the kind of positive experiences that constantly require most of our attention while we're attending to them. But perhaps time spent doing fun and thought-engaging activities with close friends may be the next best thing to the positive experience that lasts for ever?[34]

Only time will tell, I suppose.

CHAPTER 7

JUST AS LONG AS I'M NOT THE ONLY ONE

If there's one word in this book that an average sceptic wouldn't like, it's probably the word *average* – and here, when I say average, I mean average across everyone in the same country or data set. Money buys little happiness, on average. The average effect of unemployment on our happiness is negative and large. On average, time heals most wounds, but not completely for all.

But how many of us are actually *average*? Well, as it turns out, not that many.

For example, the average person in Britain taken from the nationally-representative British Household Panel Survey data set is a 45-year-old mother of one with a full-time job. And she also happens to be from Scotland.

Does that fit your description? Not if you're a man, of course. And that's almost half the UK population already.

'Well, then', a sceptic would retort, 'if I'm certainly not one of the averages, I don't see why the standard happiness results should apply to me. I personally believe that money will buy me a lot of happiness – you can give me that instead of a good friendship any day. And I don't worry about unemployment either. It wouldn't bother me at all.'

And to a certain extent, he'd be right.

* * *

One of the world's most famous economists, Chicago-based Steven Levitt, and his *Freakonomics* and *Superfreakonomics* co-author, the *New York Times* journalist Stephen Dubner, work with averages for a living. According to the two, while most of us are rarely the typical person in any given data set,

> ... knowing what happens on average is a good start. By so doing, we insulate ourselves from the tendency to build our thinking – our daily decisions, our laws, our governance – on exceptions and anomalies rather than on reality.[1]

And so it seems that averages do contain valuable information about the rules that guide our motivations and behaviours. They represent what happens in the bigger scheme of things. But the sceptic is also right when he says that there are exceptions to the rules, ones that may even be systematically pre-determined. What this means, of course, is that we should never generalise the results. Imagine the effect of relative status on happiness, for example. At the moment, it's assumed that the findings on ranking – i.e., that we care about relative position *per se* – can be generalised for everyone in the studied population.

But what if instead of having the same effect across gen-ders, men actually derive *marginally* more satisfaction than do women from being ranked higher than their peers financially – in other words, while both genders may care about ranking *per se*, a unit move in the ranking (e.g. from being ranked 22nd to 21st in the salary table within the company) will yield more satisfaction for men than it does for women? If this information isn't realised, then we would never know that, when it comes to keeping up with the Joneses, men will actually go to much greater lengths compared to women, simply because it gives them more satisfaction per unit gain.

So, yes, there are definitely exceptions to the rules. But one hypothesis is that these exceptions are just as likely to be systematic and distinguishable between people with different personal characteristics.

Like those of men and women, for example.

Exceptions to the bigger picture

It's pretty well established that, on average, we react badly to unemployment. Yet what is perhaps less known is that unemployment affects men and women differently. As it turns out, unemployment hurts more psychologically – almost twice as much – for men than for women (as is also evident from our diagram of adaptation to unemployment shown in the previous chapter). Marriage, by contrast, has been found to mean a lot more to women than to men. In America, while white men are generally significantly less satisfied with life compared to white women, the happiness gap by gender between black men and black women is almost zero. However, black men continue to be less happy with life compared to white men, and black women continue to be less happy with life compared to white women. And men enjoy sex more than women: the happiness associated with having sex four or more times a week is around one third larger for men than it is for women.

It's not only by gender that we find these stark differences in the well-being impacts of the same life events. Take education, for example. Unemployment seems to hurt the highly educated – people with more than twelve years of education – more than it does people with lower education – those with twelve years or less. Another stark difference is that, in America, each dollar buys less happiness for people with higher education than people with lower education. Moreover, each additional year of education is associated with slightly more happiness for the younger cohort (those under 40) than for the older cohort (aged 40 or older).[2]

These descriptions of some of the happiness findings show why it might be worth sometimes thinking on a smaller scale, looking at things at the sub-sample level. The overall average rules may not always apply perfectly and constantly for everyone involved in the data set.

Put simply, even if some experiences seem to matter for everyone on average, it's possible that they may mean more for some groups of people than others.

Misery loves company

We know that people care a great deal about relative position in society: the higher our status compared to other people with whom we normally compare ourselves (e.g. colleagues, friends and neighbours), the happier we seem to be with our lives overall. Here, more money gives us an extra hit of happiness if it allows a downward comparison to be made. We might even be able to say that, for two people with the same personal characteristics and earning the same income, each additional £ on top of current income will mean more happiness for the person who lives in a neighbourhood where everyone else is poorer, compared to the one who lives in a neighbourhood where everyone else is richer.

In a way, this sounds like another exception to the 'bigger picture' rule: not only has money bought more happiness on average, but each additional £ also contributes more happiness to some groups of people (in this case, those living in neighbourhoods where everyone else is poorer) than others (those living in neighbourhoods where everyone else is richer). In other words, a good experience is considered an even better experience if we're able to compare it to those who are like us in almost every way but slightly less fortunate.

Yet could there be other types of comparisons that work just as well in reverse? To put it another way, could there be some types of comparisons that can make a bad life event, when compared to others, seem less bad to us?

* * *

At the time of writing this book, one of the most eagerly awaited events is the 19th FIFA World Cup in South Africa. Held every four years since 1930, the football World Cup attracts an audience of millions around the world. The event is also very good for the economy of the host country, drawing hundreds of thousands of visitors, raking in money from abroad and boosting tourism in the process.

And as the event is drawing ever closer, information about the host country South Africa is beginning to be heavily searched and visited on the internet by those planning their trips there this summer. Where to stay? Where are all the stadiums located? What are the best hotels in Cape Town and Johannesburg? Who are the footballers representing South Africa? And among those websites providing everything we need to know about the host nation, over 70,000 people have so far chosen to visit one in particular: a website created by Malan Jacobs that, prior to 2010, was virtually unknown to the rest of the world.

Now, Malan is neither a world-class footballer nor the captain of the South African national team. He doesn't own one of the best hotels in Johannesburg or work for the South African tourist board. He's a 21-year-old student from the University of Stellenbosch. And in fact, his website says almost nothing about the upcoming World Cup in South Africa. But it certainly carries important and attention-grabbing information about his beloved country: its domestic crime rates.

TrueCRIMExpo is one of Malan's proudest achievements,[3] created when he was only seventeen. Since August 2006, the website has been reporting crime incidents in South Africa almost on a daily basis, and in an unbiased manner. As part of its campaign, which aims to generate a balanced debate on the current crime situation and to promote solutions to the problem, the website also encourages crime victims from different parts of the country to share their own experiences and thoughts, or just to vent their anger at South Africa's appallingly high crime rate (according to the United Nations Office on Drugs and Crime statistics published in 2002, South Africa has one of the highest rates of murder, assault, rape and burglary in the world).[4]

Browsing through Malan's website would give any potential visitor to South Africa a daunting experience. One report describes the robbing of 47 tourists at a guesthouse in Cape Town. Another recounts the murder of a friend of one of the website's contributors, brutally shot five times by gang members. One tells of an Austrian tourist shot and killed for his mobile phone in Durban. In one of the more recent posts, a woman in her 40s and a three-year-old child were murdered and raped in the course of one week only a few houses apart in Pretoria. The list goes on.

Many people, especially South Africans living locally and abroad, praise Malan's hard work and his valiant attempt to 'put the truth out there'. There are also many others who are, perhaps understandably, less appreciative. Even though Malan's website is intended to promote South Africa to the rest of the world by being as honest as possible about the crime problem (but showing that he and other South Africans are definitely doing something about it), many people fear that it will have an adverse effect on tourism. First impressions are everything, they say, and sometimes ignorance is bliss.

But is it really?

In 2005, I published a study reporting on the effects of being a crime victim – of burglaries and murders of loved ones – on people's happiness in South Africa.[5] The main result is hardly surprising: crime victims are extremely unhappy with their lives compared to non-victims. The psychological effect of crime is huge: using the shadow pricing method described in Chapter 5, an additional 97,000 South African rand (currently around £8,760 or $12,950) per month is required to compensate an average person for becoming a crime victim. Comparing it to the estimated effects of other life events like unemployment and education, crime ranks first on the list in terms of the magnitude of its effects.

But can there be some people who are hurt less by crime compared to others? You bet!

First, it should be noted that the estimated effect of crime reported above is based on an average crime rate of 8.5 per cent across the entire population sample. That is, for every 100 people in the data set (which was collected in 1998), 8.5 had reported being the victims of crime. If, however, we divide this average crime rate of 8.5 per cent across the entire sample by magistrate districts in South Africa and observe how it interplays with the effect of crime on people's well-being, something remarkable happens. First, we find that life is much tougher psychologically for non-victims living in regions where the crime rate on other people living in the same area is high. For these people there's a considerable amount of fear and anxiety about becoming the next victims. And yet although crime hurts our psyche a great deal, its negative effect diminishes, not dramatically but still noticeably, as the crime rate in the area goes up.

In other words, becoming a crime victim will not hurt as much in areas where the crime rate on others is already high, compared to areas where the crime rate is low. This is the case even when everything else – e.g. income, marital status, number of children, education level – is held the same across everyone in the entire sample.

Economists call the effect of other people's crime rate on the victims' well-being 'positive externality'. I call it another way of finding comfort in collective deprivation.[6] We're all in the same boat.

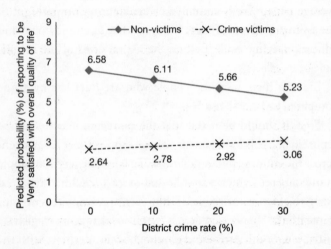

Figure 16. As the crime rate at the magistrate district level goes up, the happiness gap between crime victims and non-victims noticeably reduces.

These findings have also led to many perverse, often unthinkable, conclusions – one in particular being that, in order to make crime more tolerable for everyone in a nation, perhaps more crime should be encouraged.

But for every cloud, there's a silver lining. The presence of a positive externality from other crime victims who happen to be living locally (the fact that crime victims suffer less psychologically from victimisation in regions where crime rates are higher) essentially implies that it may be a good idea to combine crime prevention programmes – such as increased police activity, neighbourhood watch – with a programme that allows crime victims in the area to benefit from the externalities linked to other victims' experiences. For example, this can be done by encouraging better contacts among victims, especially in areas where there's asymmetrical information about other crime victims, or where there's no centralised victim support unit for victims to meet up should they want to.

And perhaps Malan's website is the first step towards achieving that goal.

The theory of social customs

George Akerlof is no ordinary economist. Eight pages long, his CV contains some amazing achievements and accolades – professor in economics at Berkeley, Nobel laureate in economics in 2001, director of the National Bureau of Economic Research, and associate editor of two of the most prestigious economic journals: the *American Economic Review* and *Quarterly Journal of Economics*. But among his hundreds of publications, he's perhaps best known to other economists for his work on the market for lemons, in which there exists asymmetrical information regarding the quality of a product between buyers and sellers.[7] For example, in the market for used cars there are both good-quality cars and bad-quality cars ('lemons'). If the true quality of a car is known only to the sellers and not to the buyers, then the buyers' best guess for a given car will be that it's of average quality. Consequently, the buyers will be willing to pay the price of a car of known average quality only, thus making the sellers of good-quality cars unable to get a high enough price to make the selling worthwhile. In other words, owners of good used cars will not place them on the used-car market. The bads, as they say in these cases, drive out the goods from the market.

But perhaps more relevant to the content of this chapter, George Akerlof is also well known for his theoretical contributions on how social customs work and how they can be linked to how we evaluate how happy we are.

Published in the *Quarterly Journal of Economics* in 1980, the 'theory of social customs' describes how, in any given society, there are many social customs whose disobedience in the right circumstances can lead to pecuniary gains for the person who disobeys.[8] However, the cost associated with disobeying – whether in the loss of reputation or the feeling of guilt for not following the custom – is smaller if disobedience is more common. Take the market for pirate DVDs in developing countries, for example. One explanation for the existence of a large and uncontrolled market for pirate DVDs in these countries may be that, at the beginning, when there were only a few suppliers of pirate DVDs in the black market, there were clear financial gains to be made for people who became suppliers, provided of course that there was sufficient demand for their knock-off DVDs. But that also came with a large cost, one being the loss of reputation in the society (who would like to be associated with a criminal, even if the crime of selling pirate DVDs seems relatively petty compared to other types of crime like robbery and murder?).

So why did they do it? Why did these few individuals choose to sell pirate DVDs in the first place if there was a loss of reputation involved? Well, one hypothesis is that, given that most pirate DVD suppliers in developing countries often come from poor families with low educational backgrounds, the thought of easy money may have outweighed the fear of losing precious reputation for these few individuals, who may not have had much of a reputation to begin with.

Over time, however, the slowly increasing number of suppliers made the sin of not following the social custom less serious for others, thus leading to more people entering the market. This continued until a critical mass or, to borrow Malcolm Gladwell's terminology, a 'tipping point' was reached, at which point the number of suppliers exploded at an exponential rate. And the reason for this? Well, now that virtually everyone is a supplier, the associated loss in reputation from becoming just another one of the suppliers is almost negligible. And once that happens, anyone – rich or poor – may take it upon themselves to sell pirate DVDs (unless, of course, the pecuniary gain from selling them has also completely disappeared too, thus leading to no more suppliers entering the market).

But there's another important implication to Akerlof's theory. If there is stigma, or shame, or even unhappiness associated with being different, then there should be no stigma or shame or unhappiness associated with being different once the 'different' has turned into the 'norm'. And this is perhaps what happens to the effect of crime on happiness: being a crime victim hurts, but it hurts less when we realise we're not the only one.

But is the varying effect of crime on well-being by others' experiences of crime the only consequence of Akerlof's theory?

Not if Andrew Clark has anything to say about it.

Unemployment and obesity as social norms

One quarter of the psychonomists, Andrew Clark has been exploring what makes people happy practically all his adult life. Born in 1963 in England, he completed his first degree at the University of Warwick before embarking on a research degree at the London School of Economics under the supervision of Andrew Oswald. Constantly knocked back by various economics journals at the start of his career, it took him several years to convince his peers that what he was doing was worthwhile and important to economics and to the understanding of human motivations in general. Now a full research professor at the Paris School of Economics, he has published more than 30 papers since 1994 on the subject of happiness alone, a feat that few economists can match.

Attracted by George Akerlof's model of social customs, Andrew Clark took it upon himself to check whether the idea could be applied to the study of the unemployment effect on our mental well-being. In particular, he wanted to find out whether the negative effect of unemployment on human happiness is smaller for some groups of people than others.[9]

And sure enough, it is.

Using the nationally-representative longitudinal data set for Britain, he found that although the unemployed were more psychologically agitated (e.g., couldn't sleep, had lost confidence, felt unhappy) almost on a daily basis compared to the employed, the well-being gap between these two groups was *smaller* in regions where the unemployment rate was high. And this well-being gap would disappear completely if the regional unemployment rate ever hit 24 per cent.

But that's not all. It appears that the unemployment norm doesn't exist only at the regional level. Strangely enough, the unemployed seem to derive some joy (or rather, consolation) from knowing that their wife or husband is unemployed as well.

So, it looks as if misery really does love company after all.[10]

And so, psychologically, crime hurts, but hurts less when there's more of it around. The same goes for unemployment. But could there be other types of social norm effect, less extreme in comparison to crime and unemployment but nevertheless more relevant in our daily lives?

Yes, of course – and one of them concerns how we perceive our body weight.

According to a recent study by Andrew Oswald, David Blanchflower and Bert Van Landegham, highly educated people are more likely to view themselves as overweight – at any given actual weight – than people of lower education.[11] What this means is that people have different comparison groups: the highly educated hold themselves to a thinner standard. The study also found that we're happier when the average weight of other people like us (of the same age, gender, and country) is higher, holding our weight constant. In other words, there's evidence that well-being is higher among those who are relatively – not merely absolutely – thin.

The social norm effect generated by other people's weight isn't limited to other people of the same age group and gender as us. Andrew Clark and his French colleague, Fabrice Etilé, show that higher BMI (body mass index = weight in kilograms divided by height in metres squared) is associated with lower life satisfaction. But it hurts marginally less psychologically for the overweight to gain one more unit of weight (i.e. a kilogram) when their spouse is also overweight or obese.[12] In simple terms, it feels okay to be fat when our loved ones – or other people with whom we normally identify – are fat as well.

But again, why on earth should we care about this? Yes, social norms matter to how things affect our happiness. But so what? So what if the average rules don't always apply to everyone in society? Are there any practical reasons why we should be concerned about this phenomenon?

Well, for one thing, it certainly has a huge implication for our motivations and behaviours.

Consider the effect of the unemployment norm on the unemployeds' well-being. Andrew Clark's results imply that life as an unemployed person isn't so bad when other people we know are also unemployed. And given that happiness is one of the most primitive human motivations there is (everyone wants to be happy and stay happy, right?), why should a relatively happy unemployed person go in search of another job when unemployment isn't the devil it was cracked up to be? Now imagine that every unemployed person in the area thinks the same way. If that's the case, then who would put any effort into searching for a job any more? It's therefore possible that unemployment is voluntary rather than involuntary in areas where unemployment is the going norm.

And so, yes, perhaps other people's miseries provide the kind of cold comfort we seek in order to cope with many of the unfortunate events in our lives, to make them seem alright. But, for some, they also have the ability to generate unwanted disincentives when seen from society's point of view. If unemployment feels okay, then there's no additional incentive (other than income) to look for a job. Or if being overweight doesn't seem to affect how we feel about ourselves all that much, then losing weight seems pointless and hard work – even though objectively- and absolutely-speaking, both having a job and having a healthy weight range are beneficial to us and to society in the long run. This partly explains why there are persistently high unemployment rates in some areas and not in others, and why there's a continuing rise in obesity among some groups of people and not others.[13]

So, the important question here is: how do we turn an already bad norm into a good norm? For instance, is there a way to make being healthy or holding a secure job the norm in a society made up of people who are overweight or who have chosen to be unemployed voluntarily?

Well, yes, there is; although it's not without controversy. But it could be extremely cheap, and could take as little (or as much) as listening to a radio programme.

Making the world a better place the controversial way

Betsy Levy Paluck has an ambition: she wants to rid the world of all prejudice and conflict in the most cost-effective way possible. A gifted psychologist, she graduated with a Ph.D. in social psychology from Yale and is now assistant professor of psychology at Woodrow Wilson School of Public and International Affairs, Princeton University. Since 2007, she has been conducting thought-provoking field-experimental research on how mass media can be used to shape prejudiced beliefs and norms among people living in the Rwandan communities in Africa.[14]

Rwanda, of course, is a country damaged by the terrible event that took place in 1994. The Rwanda genocide saw the mass killing of over 500,000 of Rwanda's Tutsis by the Hutu-dominated government under the Hutu Power ideology in the span of only 100 days. Now that it's over, Rwandans today face a crisis of trust, as survivors, returned refugees and accused killers are obliged to live side by side in their old communities. And understandably, hatreds continue to be harboured by Rwandans on both sides more than fifteen years after the killings.

Betsy's plan was to see whether she could change people's prejudiced beliefs and their perceptions of social norms through the medium of radio. To do this, she randomly assigned participating Rwandans to listen to two different radio programmes, one about health (the control group), the other the reconciliation drama *New Dawn*, an educational soap opera designed to address the mistrust, lack of communication and interaction, and trauma left by the genocide (the treatment group). What she found was something rather special. Although the rec-onciliation programme listened to by the people in the treat-ment group didn't do much to change their personal beliefs (for example, they didn't personally believe that intermarriage would bring peace), it did wonders to improve their perceptions of the going norms in their society (for instance, they would tell their children to reject the idea of in-group marriage – that is, marriage within their own regional, religious or ethnic group). They empathised a great deal more than those in the control group with real-life Rwandan prisoners, genocide survivors, poor people, and political leaders. In addition, the treatment group believed that most people in Rwandan society think that it's not naive to trust others – something that, unfortunately, people in the control group didn't believe in as much.

And so it seems that we can turn a bad norm into a good one, at least in terms of people's perceptions about the going norms in the society. But Betsy also notes that personal beliefs may be extremely difficult to change, and norms may influence people's happiness vis-à-vis their motivations and behaviours only if they come with a salient and normative pressure to conform – a system of 'Don't do that! You'll be frowned upon', perhaps.

She ends her study with a sobering thought: If a good norm that promotes good behaviours can be generated out of thin air by the media and other sources, so could bad norms. Something the Rwandans know only too well.[15]

What Betsy has been able to show through the clever use of a radio programme is that people's perceptions of norms can be changed fairly easily and cheaply. But what about behav-iours? Can we use an artificially-generated norm to influence our behaviours (or as economists would call them, our 'revealed preferences') for the better?

One of the ongoing political challenges in the world today is trying to find the most cost-effective way to combat climate change. The UK government, for instance, has been using TV commercials to convey messages of the dangers of global warming to the public in the hope that they will conform. Switch off the light when it's not being used, they say. Don't leave things on standby. You can save the world. Do it for your children and their children.

The UK government's strategy, of course, is to generate fear among the general public. Fear for the survival of our future generations. Fear for mankind. Fear for the earth itself. What could be a better motivator than fear?

But has it worked? Has the government been successful in creating a social norm of 'switching off to save the environment' among us?

I doubt it.

One reason for my scepticism is what economists call the 'coordination problem'. For one thing, there's no clear mechanism as to how society can punish those who leave their electricity running at night (who outside our home is going to know that we leave our TV on standby 24 hours a day?). The commercials also couldn't say anything about *how many* people exactly are doing their bit for the environment, and exactly *who they are*. What this means is that there's almost no cost, at least not one that can be inflicted by society upon our conscience (i.e. no loss of reputation), from disobeying the rules. But we may believe it. We may believe that the world has changed for the better, that people all over the world are now doing all they can to help save the environment. And yet, perhaps no differently to what Betsy found in her studies of Rwandans, our personal beliefs may have remained just the same as before we were exposed to the government's warnings of the dangers of global warming.

And so the chances are that we'll continue to behave in exactly the same way, believing that if we don't do it – if we don't switch things off at night – other people around the globe will surely do their part. The only problem with this is that everybody else will probably think the same, which will lead to only small changes in the average usage of energy pre- and post-commercials.

In short, while perceptions about how much the world is concerned about the state of the environment may have changed for the people who have been exposed to the commercials, their behaviours may have remained the same as before. This raises the question: how then can we generate the kind of norms that come with a clear enough pressure to conform and so potentially have some kind of impact on our behaviour? Three behavioural scientists, Noah Goldstein of the University of Chicago, Robert Cialdini of Arizona State University, and Vladas Griskevicius of the University of Minnesota, have made a novel attempt to find out.[16]

In keeping with global environmental programmes that encourage people to save energy, many hotels now urge their customers to re-use their towels during their stay, helping to conserve resources and reduce the amount of detergent-related pollutants released into the environment. And they do this by strategically placing a card in customers' bathrooms that says: 'HELP SAVE THE ENVIRONMENT. You can show your respect for nature and help save the environment by reusing your towels during your stay.' A message not very different to the one shown to us by the government commercials on TV.

But does it work?

Even when there's clear monitoring of towel usage in place (hotel workers normally check the rate of usage regardless of whether there's an environmental programme in place), the results on people's behaviours from the introduction of the 'HELP SAVE THE ENVIRONMENT' sign in their bathrooms have been far from satisfactory: only about 35 per cent of hotel customers conform to the environmental message by reusing their towel. That's probably no different to the percentage of people who react to the commercials on the TV.

So, to try to increase the effectiveness of the environmental messages, the three behavioural scientists came up with an idea to include different norm messages on the cards to be placed in customers' bathrooms. For example, one of their designs included a message that said:

JOIN YOUR FELLOW GUESTS IN HELPING TO SAVE THE ENVIRONMENT. In a study conducted in Fall 2003, 75% of the guests participated in our new resource savings programme by using their towels more than once. You can join your fellow guests in this programme to help save the environment by reusing your towels during your stay.

The card, aimed at eliciting the general feeling among customers that there exists a social custom obeyed by the majority of guests who stay at the hotel, did the trick: almost 45 per cent of hotel guests exposed to this message ended up using their towel more than once – a near 10 per cent increase from the standard 'HELP SAVE THE ENVIRONMENT' message. Similar re-usage rates of approximately 45 per cent were obtained when the messages on the cards were changed to 'JOIN YOUR FELLOW CITIZENS IN SAVING THE ENVIRONMENT' and 'JOIN

THE MEN AND WOMEN WHO ARE HELPING TO SAVE THE ENVIRONMENT'. But the most effective message of all, with a towel re-usage rate of almost 50 per cent, contained the following message:

> JOIN YOUR FELLOW GUESTS IN HELPING TO SAVE THE ENVIRONMENT. In a study conducted in Fall 2003, 75% of the guests **who stayed in this room** participated in our resource savings programme by using their towels more than once. You can join your fellow guests in this programme to help save the environment by reusing your towels during your stay.

And so, what Goldstein, Cialdini and Griskevicius have been able to show is that artificially-generated norms of pro-social behaviours can *really* shape people's behaviours for the better, provided that a meaningful social identity (i.e. those with whom we identify ourselves the most) can also be made salient when the messages of good behaviours are being established. And as it turns out, the most effective normative appeal in their study was one that described the group behaviour that occurred in the setting that most closely matched the individuals' immediate situational circumstances: the norms (or average behaviours) of those who stayed in the same room as them.

Their results make intuitive sense. While it may be difficult for us to identify ourselves with the rest of the world, we're more likely to change our behaviours to match the average behaviours of other people *like us* – whether it's the same age group, same gender, or same citizenship – as well as those who have been through the same situation we are currently facing and ended up behaving in a certain way.

And so, it seems that while knowing what happens on average provides a useful benchmark for what would make us happy and what would not, there may well be exceptions to the generalisation. Something may hurt us more than it hurts others, while other things may mean more to other people than they mean to us. Nevertheless, all these exceptions to the average rules aren't entirely unpredictable; for one thing, the amount of happiness (or unhappiness) that can be experienced from a life event or an activity may depend largely on how the event or the activity is viewed by the majority of people in the society – whether it's approved or frowned upon. And because of this close link between 'what I think' and 'what the society thinks', social scientists believe that we can encourage pro-social behaviours by simply moderating people's perceptions of what the current norms are to match how we want them to behave.

But if that's the case, if we can really manipulate people's perceptions of norms and consequently their well-being and behaviours at will, would it be entirely ethical to do so? What would the public say if they found out they had been – to borrow Richard Thaler and Cass Sunstein's term – 'nudged' by the government to do something they would never normally do, even if that something was beneficial to them on multiple levels?[17]

Would they still be happy about it?

CHAPTER 8

FOCUSING ILLUSIONS

The ironic thing about being a happiness researcher is that we spend half our time telling people why what they believe will make them happy may be wrong. Conventional wisdom tells us that money buys happiness, you'd say. Yes, but not as much as you think it will, we'd respond. Children are God's gifts, and every day has been a better, happier day since I had my kids, you'd declare. Yeah, but you'd probably be just as happy if you didn't have them, we'd reply. I'll never get over the death of my husband, it's just too painful, you'd cry. Give it a year or two, we'd say.

And that's why there's a joke about why you should never invite a happiness researcher to a funeral. There's a chance that he'd ruin it for everyone else.

But joking aside (most happiness researchers do the right thing at funerals and withhold what we typically find in various data sets regarding the quick and full recovery from the death of loved ones), could it be that we, the happiness researchers, are wrong? I know it's difficult to argue against hard data, but what else would explain why there's such a large discrepancy between our intuitions and what the numbers in the data are telling us?

* * *

I woke up with a start.

That doesn't normally happen to me, but on that first day of spring in 2009, it did. It was 20 March, only two days before

Mother's Day here in the UK. I looked at my alarm clock. It's only 8.00am. There's no teaching today. Lie in. You deserve it.

Then the phone started ringing.

'Hello?'

'Hello. Is that Dr Natta…wood Powdatavee?'

'Yes, this is he.' It had been almost five years to the day since I stopped trying to correct journalists when they mispronounce my name. 'And you can call me Nick.'

'Hi Nick. This is —— from Channel Five. Just thought we'd let you know that we'll be discussing the research you published in the *Psychologist* yesterday about why children don't make you happy in *The Wright Stuff* in about an hour?'

'Oh, okay. Thank you,' I said, hanging up the phone.

An hour later, still in my pyjamas, I was downstairs in the living room, eager to see what other people had to say about the study. I watched in horror as the discussion panel on *The Wright Stuff* (a typical weekday morning chat show) spent most of their time telling the audience how stupid I was. 'What does this doctor know about raising a child?' one of the panellists said. 'He's an idiot. Of course kids make you happy. He probably doesn't have any children himself. Or if he does, his children will probably hate him for publishing this rubbish.'

The day went by in a blur. The *Daily Mail* published the findings of the study that same morning under the inflammatory headline, 'Children don't make you happy … says an expert who doesn't have any', which attracted almost 100 online comments from parents (mostly angry ones) across the British Isles.[1] 'What does he know? He doesn't even have any children.' There were similar reactions from readers of the *New York Times* when journalist and family life blogger Lisa Belkin devoted a page on her website to describing the results.[2] And even around ten radio interviews later, I still felt numbed by the reactions from the general public, who phoned in to let me know what they thought about my findings, and generally where I could shove them.

Although there were a handful of people (mainly non-parents) who agreed with the findings, the publication in the *Psychologist*[3] seemed to have generated a mini media storm around Mother's Day. Over the next few weeks, I received several emails from people around the globe telling me how wrong I was. I even received a card from a churchgoer in America telling me I should repent for what I believe. A close personal friend suggested jokingly that I should leave the country for a few days. Feeling overwhelmed, I decided to send the published paper to Dan Gilbert – the author of *Stumbling on Happiness* – and I shared with him the public's reactions. He wrote back within hours:

> Thanks, Nick. This is great. I don't do research on this topic but I do sometimes mention these findings in public talks, and I also get hate mail every time I do. Nothing I've ever said has raised as much ire. Be prepared! —d.

I felt much better after reading Dan's email, not only because he always knows exactly what to say to make you feel better (he is, after all, one of the world's best social psychologists), but because his experience and my experience are clearly mutual: most people find the results – that on average children don't make us happy or keep us happy – incredibly *surprising*, not to say offensive.

The question is: Why?

Is it because all of us who believe that children really bring us significantly more joy than misery are classic exceptions to the average rules, that we are all somehow outliers in the data sets? Possibly. But let's think about that for a moment.

First, there's evidence. And overwhelming evidence too, with one of the first examples appearing in print as early as 1957.[4] The conclusions have been stark and consistent: in America, there's substantial evidence that, on average, the presence of a child or children in the family lowers marital satisfaction for the parents. However, when these parents are asked how they perceive that their children affect their marital lives, the majority conclude that their children have affected their marital happiness in the most positive way possible.[5]

Why the inconsistency? Are these parents afraid to tell the truth when it comes to how their children have affected their married life? That's one possibility.

Besides, one might argue that the negative effect of children on marital satisfaction – as long as the results weren't obtrusively obtained (i.e. by asking directly how parents perceive the effect of children) – isn't completely unpredictable anyway. Sure, many people will find it hard to admit even to themselves – let alone the person interviewing them – that their children have adversely affected their marital life, but maybe the evidence that parents tend to report lower levels of marital satisfaction than non-parents is already intuitively obvious? Kids can undoubtedly be whiny. They also need constant attention from parents, which is something that used to be shared only by the two people in the relationship. And since questions on marital satisfaction are domain-specific, aimed to elicit our feelings about the way we think our marriage is going (it's like asking how happy we are with our spouse), maybe the negative effect on the reported marital satisfaction of parents could have been expected. But the effect of children on parents' *overall* happiness or life satisfaction, which is supposed to capture all the things we cherish dearly in our lives – ergo, our children – must be positive, right? Perhaps all we need to do to get the desired result is to ask the right question.

The trouble with this is that the evidence still doesn't back up our intuitions about the link between children and happiness: while there are a few exceptions,[6] researchers continue to observe similar patterns of parents reporting either the same or lower happiness, life satisfaction, and mental well-being compared to non-parents in general.[7] It's the same in Britain as in America or Germany. Furthermore, there's also evidence that the strains associated with parenthood are not only limited to the period during which children are physically and economically dependent: older parents whose children have left home report being only as happy as, or slightly unhappier than, non-parents of similar age and status.[8] More recently, research using the day reconstruction method (DRM) – which asks individuals to recall memories of the previous day by constructing a diary consisting of a sequence of episodes of what they were doing, who they were with, and what they were feeling at the time of the experience – finds that while interaction with one's children ranks first among enjoyable activities, taking care of one's children also ranks just above the least enjoyable activities of working, housework and commuting.[9] There is thus a clear conflict between what we believe ('I enjoy my kids') and specific episode reports of happiness ('But they were a pain last night'), which could partly explain why parents are no different to non-parents – or, in some cases, less happy compared to non-parents – when it comes to their moment-to-moment happiness.

But one argument, of course, would be that parents and non-parents are systematically different in terms of their personal characteristics and personality traits. Perhaps non-parents in the data are just born happier than those with children, thus making them seem happier without a child. But if these non-parents ever decide to become parents themselves, surely children will bring more joy to their lives than they could possibly imagine? This is a fair point; it also ties in very well with the estimated positive shadow price of the birth of a child (£2,500 per annum in the first year) discussed in Chapter 5 of this book. And to solve this problem, what one could do is track the same individuals through time before and after the birth of their child. In other words, instead of comparing happiness between parents and non-parents, we could just compare happiness *before* and *after* having children. We could then see whether having children is associated with a within-person rise in happiness in general.

But to our surprise, even when we have tracked people's happiness for significant periods before and after the birth of their child, there seems to be no evidence whatsoever of a continuing rise in happiness (or life satisfaction) in the years that followed the momentous event.[10] In fact, as is evidently clear in the diagram of life satisfaction in the years before and after the birth of a child presented in Chapter 6 (Figure 15), our life satisfaction even declines noticeably one year after the child's birth, and it remains negative until the child is roughly five years old. Furthermore, these results are hardly a one-off: the dynamic of life satisfaction before and after having children is the same for both male and female parents.[11]

If you're now shouting abuse at me, then it might be worth considering that perhaps you really are an outlier. Maybe you don't fall within the statistical boundaries that led to the conclusion that children don't generally bring significantly more happiness to us. Put another way, if 90 per cent of the people who were surveyed became no happier after having children, and 5 per cent became completely depressed after having children, then you *must* fall within the other 5 per cent who became absolutely elated after having children.

But how can the majority of people fall within that 5 per cent of the sampled population? It just doesn't seem to make much sense (remember that, more often than not, the data sets are nationally-representative). It's also worth noting that this highly improbable circumstance bears resemblance to one of the conclusions reached by three US-based economists, Günter Hitsch and Ali Hortaçsu of the University of Chicago, and Dan Ariely of MIT, in a study of online dating.[12] Using a sample of 3,004 men and 2,783 women in Boston and San Diego, they found that, incredibly, many of these people are extremely good-looking. Or at least they said they are. For example, 19 per cent of men and 24 per cent of women said they possess 'very good looks', while 49 per cent of men and 48 per cent of women have 'above average looks'. Only a minority – 29 per cent of men and 26 per cent of women – said that they 'look like anyone else walking on the street'. This leaves only *1 per cent* of users with 'less than average looks', and a few who avoid the question altogether and joke that a date should 'bring a bag just in case mine tears'. All of this raises a question: Is it really the case that the online dating world is over-represented by people who are either extremely good-looking or above-average-looking?[13]

It's possible (for instance, better-looking people may select themselves to online dating more than worse-looking people), although most would probably agree that it's highly unlikely.

So, perhaps like some of the supposedly 'very good-looking' users of online dating websites, the majority of parents also lie through their teeth when they say that children have made them feel happier than ever before?

Not necessarily. How can it be a lie when they really believe that that's how they feel: that children really make them a happier person every day?

Rejecting the data

There's no denying the fact that there's a widespread belief in every human culture that children bring happiness. When people are asked to think about parenthood – either imagining future offspring or thinking about their current ones – most tend to conjure up pictures of healthy babies, handsome boys and gorgeous girls who are flawless in every way. This is the case even when the prospective parents know that raising a child will be painfully difficult; they tend to think happily about parenthood, which is why most of them eventually leap into it.

So what explains why many of us have such a rosy view of parenthood, and get extremely angry if other people suggest otherwise? Perhaps working in the same way as Richard Dawkins' concept of memes – intergenerational transmissions of ideas that are similar to the passing of genes from parents to children – the belief that 'children bring happiness' transmits itself much more successfully from generation to generation than the belief that 'children bring misery'. This phenomenon, which Daniel Gilbert calls a 'super-replicator',[14] can be explained further by the fact that people who believe that there's no joy in parenthood – and who thus stop having children – are less likely to pass on their beliefs beyond their own generation.

In other words, only the beliefs that have the best chance of transmission, even if they are faulty ones, will be passed on.

So from the evolutionary perspective, it seems entirely viable to think that at least prospective parents would believe that having children will make them much happier than if they were to remain child-free. But how to explain the majority of parents who appear to be no happier than non-parents but who say that children really bring happiness?

It may be due partly to our natural desire to be – or at least appear to be – one with the norm, both consciously and subconsciously. Research on 'social desirability' bias has shown that people have the tendency to over-report good behaviours/ attitudes or under-report bad behaviours/attitudes so that they will be viewed favourably in the eyes of others.[15] Because of this need to please, some parents may respond to the question, 'Are you a happier person since you became a parent?', that they are – even when they aren't – simply because they don't want to appear deviant from the social standards.

But that reason alone can't be it. Why? Well, as an example, it's not unusual to see parents proudly showing photos of their children to whoever wants to see them, or even without being asked. Some get really cross if they hear other parents complaining that they're more miserable now after having kids. In short, it just doesn't seem plausible that all these parents would go out of their way to lie about how they really feel about their children, or how their children make them feel.

So could there be other, more convincing reasons to explain such a discrepancy between what we really believe to be true and what the data actually say?

There are several potential theories here. According to Daniel Gilbert,[16] when we believe that something makes us happy, we're willing to pay a high price for it. But this also works in reverse: when we pay a lot for something, we're willing to believe that it gives us happiness in return. Because evolution passes on this unconditional compulsion to care for our children, we also wouldn't want to have it any other way. Given the high price we pay, it's therefore not surprising at all that we rationalise those costs and conclude that our children must be repaying us with happiness.

A complementary psychological explanation as to why many parents find this result (that children can make them unhappy) surprising and offensive can be found in the research on morality by professor of psychology at the University of Virginia and author of *The Happiness Hypothesis*,[17] Jonathan Haidt. In a work published in *Psychological Review*, he explored how our brain normally functions when it encounters a situation that seems perversely immoral to us. He did this by presenting the following scenario to his research subjects and asking them a simple question:

> Julie and Mark are brother and sister. They are travelling together in France on summer vacation from college. One night they are staying alone in a cabin near the beach. They decide that it would be interesting and fun if they tried making love. At least it would be a new experience for each of them. Julie was already taking birth control pills, but Mark uses a condom too, just to be safe. They both enjoy making love, but they decide not to do it again. They keep that night as a special secret, which makes them feel even closer to each other. What do you think about that, was it OK for them to make love?[18]

What Haidt found is that many participants in the research were visibly uncomfortable with the incestuous scenario. When asked what exactly made them feel uncomfortable, some participants justified it by saying that incestuous sex leads to offspring that suffer genetic abnormalities. At that point, Haidt would interject: 'But Julie was on birth control pills, and Mark used a condom!' But instead of conceding, the participants would carry on trying to find other arguments to justify their feelings. It's frowned upon by society, some would say. Again, he would interrupt: 'But nobody else knows about this.' The argument and counter-argument would go on until the participants ran out of justifiable reasons and simply said: 'I don't know, I can't explain it, I just know it's wrong.'

Haidt concludes that moral judgements – whether towards incest, cheating, or even people saying that children make them unhappy – aren't always caused by moral reasoning, which occurs when we engage in rationalisation before making a judgement on whether something makes moral sense to us. Instead, moral reasoning often comes *after* we have already made up our mind about the nature of the event in question.

In other words, at the first instance of witnessing or hearing something we think is wrong or abnormal, our emotional brain goes to work much faster than our ability to reason. We make snap judgements based on prior beliefs, and subsequently try to back them up with plausible reasoning. Sometimes we succeed at winning the argument. And sometimes we succumb to the fact that there are probably no rational justifications for why we should be feeling the way we do, but we still do anyway. And this partly explains why, even in the face of almost irrefutable evidence, many parents would still reject or react angrily to the news that they may be no happier than non-parents.

While these explanations sound perfectly credible, there's another, perhaps even more plausible, explanation for the counter-intuitive findings on the relationship between parenthood and happiness.

Thinking about it

According to David Schkade, professor of marketing and strategy at the University of San Diego, and Daniel Kahneman, Nobel laureate in economics and Princeton psychologist, part of the problem with stated preferences – i.e., when we say we prefer something to other things, or any judgement requiring the comparison of two or more alternatives – is that they suffer from an inherent 'focusing illusion': our tendency to exaggerate the importance of *anything* when we're focusing our attention on it, best captured in the maxim: 'Nothing in life is quite as important as you think it is while you are thinking about it.'[19] To illustrate their point, the scholars carried out a laboratory experiment on two distinct groups of participants: university students studying in California (University of California, Irvine and University of California, Los Angeles), and university students studying in the Midwest of America (University of Michigan and Ohio State University). As part of the experiment, both groups of students were asked a series of questions about their own life satisfaction, as well as how happy they thought students in California were compared to students in the Midwest.

When asked to predict whether students in California or students in the Midwest would be happier with their lives, respondents in both California and the Midwest forecasted that the former would be happier when, in fact, students in both places are actually just as satisfied with their lives as the other.

What this finding implies is that there's a common perception that people in California enjoy a much better life than people in the Midwest. This perception, as noted by Schkade and Kahneman, is anchored in the belief that the climate is much nicer in California, where the sun shines all year round, than in the Midwest, where it's often cold and icy (and it's worth noting that this belief is completely justified by the fact that students in California reported to be more satisfied with their climate than students in the Midwest). Nevertheless, contrary to their – and perhaps many other people's – intuitions, the advantages of life in California didn't seem to show up in the reported life satisfaction of those who live there.

The reason for this discrepancy appears obvious: California and the Midwest differ mostly in terms of their weather, which is salient in a joint evaluation of both places but not salient in a separate evaluation of living in one place. In other words, whenever we're prompted to think about how satisfied we are with our lives, weather hardly ever comes to our mind at all. Rather, we tend to focus our attention on other life aspects that are much more salient than the climate of where we live – things like job prospects, financial situation and personal safety, for example.

To imagine what it might be like to be a mother or father to children is perhaps not much different to imagining what it might be like to live in California: we're likely to focus more of our attention on the good things about being a parent and less on the bad things, largely because of the inherent belief that children bring happiness. What this theory implies is that we're likely to become happier with our lives – and much more so than usual because of the focusing effect – the moment we find out we are about to become a parent, which could be up to nine months before the birth of our child. Nevertheless, our happiness in the periods that follow childbirth is likely to be determined largely by how our attention is normally spent during those periods.

In terms of frequency, do we spend most of our time on cloud nine following the birth of our child? Or do we spend most of it being anxious about the well-being of our little David or Sarah?

The evidence seems to suggest the latter: from the psychonomists' diagram of leads and lags in life satisfaction before and after childbirth in Chapter 6 (Figure 15), we can clearly see that, on average, parents become significantly happier with life one year before the birth of their child – while also remaining just as happy at the year of the birth – before dropping beyond zero within one year of the child being born. Both fathers and mothers then go on to experience significant unhappiness for the next four years before being 'just' content about parenthood, i.e., they become no less happy than when they didn't have any children all those years ago.

But why is that? Where have all the positive experiences from raising a child gone? 'Yes,' you may say, 'I concede that being a parent is really hard work, but surely there must be some positive experiences that come with it to offset all those negative ones of having to change dirty nappies and the midnight wake-up call?'

'And so, yes,' you would say, 'I would probably buy the results that show no differences in happiness between parents and non-parents, but certainly *not* the findings that children bring only misery in their first few years. This is simply because I, as do most other people, believe that seeing my first-born smile for the first time would do more than enough to compensate for any stress he or she might bring me, even if the former (positive) experience is rarer than the latter (negative) experience.'

'In other words, shouldn't the well-being hit from a higher-quality but less frequent experience with our children be larger – or, at the very least, be equal to – the small but more frequent misery that raising children can bring?'

Attention!

Again, the idea of focusing illusion and how we normally allocate our attention to different activities in our lives can help explain that. For example, we tend to believe that the relatively rare but exceedingly positive experiences – such as seeing our children smile for the first time, or graduate from university, or get married – will give us massive increases in happiness. And indeed they do. Yet these boosts in well-being, often to our surprise, tend not to last for that long (see Chapter 6). One explanation for this lies in the nature of these experiences. How often on a day-to-day basis do we spend our time thinking about relatively rare but extremely positive experiences – not only about our children, but also about everything else positive that takes place in our lives – that is, if we're not prompted to think about them? Things like marriage or last year's promotion.

A common answer to this would probably be: 'Not as often as we thought we would (or should).'

Take thoughts about money, for example. According to a study published in the journal *Science* by Daniel Kahneman and colleagues, whenever people are prompted to reflect on what more money could do to their lives, they tend to think about using it to do the things they like doing, such as driving nice cars, watching a large-screen TV, or playing golf.[20] However, in reality, the scientists found that richer people in fact spend most of their time engaging in activities associated with negative experienced emotions (such as time spent being in a bad mood), but not greater experienced happiness. This includes work, compulsory non-work activities (such as shopping and childcare), and active leisure (exercise), all of which are associated with no greater happiness, on average, but with slightly higher tension and stress.

In other words, there's evidence to suggest that people tend to mispredict between what they think they would be doing and what they *actually* end up doing with most of their time after becoming richer. They still work exceptionally hard – partly to maintain that high-income status – and even engage in fewer leisure activities that, on balance, would fill them with positive emotions.

We may become extremely happy as soon as we receive a large pay rise or cash windfall (simply because we spend a lot of time in the beginning thinking about it), but soon enough that money will go into our bank account or into a spending spree in the form of things like a nice car or a big house in the country, most of which, having got them, we don't spend a lot of time thinking about any more. However, if we're asked to think about that large pay rise or windfall again, because of the focusing illusion we're likely to exaggerate the value it brings.

On the other hand, it's much more likely that we as parents will end up spending a large chunk of our time attending to the core questions of childcare, such as: 'Am I going to be able to pick up David from school on time?' 'How do I stop Sarah from crying?' Most of these experiences, as indicated in the study by Kahneman and colleagues, are associated with self-reported negative emotions. They are also perhaps a lot less salient than the positive experiences we have with our kids, which is why we tend not to attach a lot of weight to them when we're prompted with a question of whether or not children bring happiness. Nevertheless, it's these small but more frequent negative experienced emotions, rather than the relatively rarer positive experienced emotions, that take up most of the attention we are allowed in a day.

And for this reason, it should come as no surprise to us that these negative experienced emotions that come with parenthood may show up much more often in our self-reported happiness in the first few years of our child being born than activities that are, although extremely rewarding, relatively less frequent in comparison.

In addition to this, when we reflect on how children can contribute to our subjective well-being, not only do we tend to misallocate our attention towards only the good things about being a parent, we tend to forget entirely to take into account the good things about *not* being a parent: romantic time alone with our partner, a whole night's sleep, a social life with our friends, sex; most of which many parents are likely to have to sacrifice after the children have been born.[21]

So even if children do bring us plenty of happiness, life before having kids probably wasn't too bad either. Hence why, on balance, parents are not significantly happier with life than non-parents.

The subject of our motivations

These findings are, if you can bring yourself to accept them, extremely depressing. But what if we didn't give in to this comfortable belief that children bring happiness? What if all of us decided one day, for the sake of our own personal happiness, not to have children any more?

It's not even worth thinking about.

And so it's arguable that, from the evolutionary point of view, this cognitive bias (or what Kahneman and co. called focusing illusion) that we have is not only important but downright indispensable for the passing on of our genes. Without it, there might be no primal motivation for reproduction.

One remaining popular argument against the counterintuitive findings on children and happiness, and perhaps the most valid one, lies in the way happiness is measured. Sure, having children may not lead to greater day-to-day or moment-to-moment happiness, but it definitely does wonders for us in the 'a lot like happiness' box. It relates to things like meaning and self-worth.

In a day reconstruction method (DRM) study conducted by Mathew White of Plymouth University and Paul Dolan of the London School of Economics, it was found that, consistent with the study by Kahneman and colleagues, taking care of children is associated with lower pleasure experienced by the participants. However, the novel thing about their study was that they also included measures of thoughts as well as feelings. And what they found is that although time with children ranks relatively low in terms of how pleasurably the episode was spent, it was thought of as *very rewarding* compared to other, more pleasurable activities, which included rest, watching TV, and listening to music. They also found these thoughts to be important predictors of overall life satisfaction: time spent doing rewarding things is positively related with how we tend to rate our happiness.[22]

In other words, the two scholars argue that there's more than just one dimension of subjective well-being, more than just pleasure. Time spent raising children may not be so pleasurable for us, but it sure is rewarding.

At any rate, two things are clear. First, children may give us a lot of things, but a permanent increase in our day-to-day positive emotions certainly isn't one of them.

Second, as indicated by Mathew White and Paul Dolan, the 'thinking about it' part is nevertheless good for our well-being, given that thoughts are extremely important predictors of our overall life satisfaction. For this reason, we should always remind ourselves to stop and think more often about the joy of having children (and if that happened, we'd definitely begin to see children showing up more positively in the happiness data). Similarly, knowing that we were probably just as much of a pain to our parents when we were younger, perhaps it's about time we started paying them back with happiness in any way we can.

And, apparently, that's with grandchildren in my parents' case.

CHAPTER 9

WHY SHOULD WE BE HAPPY?

In his book *Happiness is Overrated*,[1] Raymond Angelo Belliotti, a distinguished teaching professor of philosophy at SUNY Fredonia, wrote that life shouldn't be all about the pursuit of pleasurable experiences and hedonic lifestyles. Rather, it should be focused on pursuing meaningful and rewarding experiences – like spending time with children, for example. And if happiness is a by-product of that, then that's great. But happiness itself should never be the goal of our motivations and behaviours.

This is simply because, more often than not, the more we search for happiness, the more it eludes us (remember the pursuit of happiness through status when other people are doing the same thing?). It's better to live life meaningfully and be unhappy than be happy from a life that has no meaning.

And yes, when he puts it that way, I couldn't agree more.

But do the majority of other people agree? Do the majority believe, like Belliotti, that happiness really is overrated?

* * *

There are literally hundreds of books on happiness for sale on Amazon.com. Some are more popular than others, and we know this from the sales rank that Amazon reports on its website. Since we economists are obsessed with studying people's revealed preferences, I thought it would be interesting – as a raw data indicator – to see how Belliotti's book on happiness ranks in terms of popularity among other non-fiction books on happiness. A little research on Amazon yields the following top five non-fiction books on happiness (as of Tuesday 20 April 2010):

Rankings (#n = sales rank among all the books on Amazon.com)[2]

1. (#116) Gretchen Rubin's *The Happiness Project*
2. (#371) Rick Hanson's *Buddha's Brain: The Practical Neuroscience of Happiness, Love, and Wisdom*
3. (#870) Richard Thaler and Cass Sunstein's *Nudge: Improving Decisions About Health, Wealth, and Happiness*
4. (#973) Lucy Danziger and Catherine Birndorf's *The Nine Rooms of Happiness: Loving Yourself, Finding Your Purpose, and Getting Over Life's Little Imperfections*
5. (#1,367) Daniel Gilbert's *Stumbling on Happiness*

What about Belliotti's book?

?. (#6,941,674) Raymond Angelo Belliotti's *Happiness is Overrated*

Obviously, there are many reasons why some books are more popular than others: for example, the quality of the publisher, the pitch, the cover of the book, how much advertising has gone into it, the content, the year of publication and how long it has been in the market, etc. Since most books on Amazon's bestseller list have recently been published, it's not at all surprising that Belliotti's book – published in 2003 – doesn't fare as well against its peers. But from the books on the list above, most of which tell us what we need to do to be happier (or, in the case of *Stumbling on Happiness*, why the things we thought would make us happier don't), one thing seems to be clear: even if we can neither accept nor reject the idea that happiness is overrated, people continue to want to know exactly how to attain it.

So are we all completely missing the point here? Is happiness really overrated by all of us, and not just Amazon's customers?

Well, let's have a look at it objectively.

Happiness as input

So far in this book, we've been treating happiness as a kind of output, something that life experiences generate to keep us motivated and focused. And while we've learnt that some experiences turn out more happiness than others – for example, a move from having no social life to seeing friends every day is worth more happiness than getting married – we've also learnt that, more often than not, happiness is fleeting and impermanent. We've also been told that money buys happiness, but perhaps not as much as we think. We've even learnt from the study by Mathew White and Paul Dolan mentioned in the last chapter that not all meaningful experiences give us happiness (e.g. time spent with children), while the experiences that give us the most pleasure often leave us feeling less than fulfilled (e.g. time spent watching TV).

No wonder Belliotti claims that happiness is overrated. Reading about what we thought would make us happy – but in reality, doesn't – could make anyone depressed. Well, that would be the case, of course, if there were no clear objective benefits (both private and public) to being happy, even just for a little while.

So are there?

* * *

Vincent Van Gogh was a misunderstood genius. Born the eldest son of a minister of the Protestant church at Zundert (province of Noord Brabant, Holland) in 1853, there were no signs of any exceptional artistic abilities during his early years. But he was definitely happy. According to the Dutch psychiatrist A.J. Westerman Holstijn:

> It seems to me that most psychiatrists who have studied Van Gogh's life do not emphasize sufficiently that

the youth Vincent was a perfectly normal, well-adapted and sociable young man, which is in sharp contrast to his bizarre and abnormal personality in his later years. In London the extravert side of his character became even more marked. Here also he did his work with enthusiasm and devotion, was agreeable and sociable, and – imagine this in relation to the later Vincent! – went daily to the city elegantly turned out in a grey top-hat! We get a definite impression of a well-adapted young man, whose career, until his 21st year, is developing smoothly and easily.[3]

Then a series of unfortunate events happened. First, Vincent had to endure the pain of rejection from a girl to whom he proposed when he was working in London. This led to him becoming extremely depressed and disillusioned about everything that surrounded him, including his initial joy in painting. He then lost his job soon after coming back home to the Netherlands. Later, he was again rejected, this time by a girl he met in Brussels. And not long after that, his father died, which sent him spiralling downwards into deep depression and grave mental illness. He also suffered constantly from anxiety and nervousness. Having had enough of life, he committed suicide in 1890 when he was only 37 years old.

And yet, during those periods of grief and despair, Vincent Van Gogh produced arguably the best works of his life. His paintings *The Potato-Eaters* and *Portrait of Dr Gachet* (which was sold for a record price of $82.5 million in 1990) are some notable examples. But perhaps the best painting he did, and one of the best known in the world today, was the view outside his room at night while he was staying in a mental asylum at St Rémy in France: *De Sterrennacht. The Starry Night.*

The link between Van Gogh's depression and his creativity is the stuff of legend. Some have even suggested that there would never have been such paintings as the *Portrait of Dr Gachet* and *The Starry Night* if Van Gogh hadn't been a tortured soul. Nevertheless, the scientific evidence on the link between creativity and mental illness has actually been rather mixed. On the one hand, studies have found depression to be associated positively with high levels of creative achievement, and that there's a higher incidence of bipolar illness and depression among creative individuals (although this applies more to artistic, rather than scientific, creativity) than that found in the general population.[4]

But why might being in a bad state or a depressive mood foster our creative buds? Well, according to psychologist Leonard Martin and colleagues, bad moods trigger the feeling that something isn't going well and more effort is therefore needed to get us out of this mess, which for some can lead to extraordinarily creative behaviours.[5]

By contrast, there have also been many studies that have found good moods to have desirable effects on creativity. For instance, professor of psychology at Cornell University Alice Isen proposes that good moods play a very positive role in our ability to think. First, they help free up some space in our brain for processing the task at hand. Second, they help defocus our attention, allowing us to think more broadly about the subject of our thoughts. And lastly, they help raise our mental flexibility, thereby increasing the probability that we will be able to associate seemingly unrelated elements in our head to form something novel and creative.[6]

Put simply, positive moods have the ability to unclutter our brain and give it additional space to think creatively.

But theories mean nothing if they have no evidence to back them up. Isen does this by showing that participants in her laboratory experiment who had been induced to be in a good mood – from either receiving a gift or seeing a funny film clip – tended to perform at a much higher level in tasks relating to creativity compared to participants in the control group. For example, people in a good mood have been found to perform significantly better than others in ingenuity tests and at exercises that require flexible problem-solving.[7] Good moods are even found to have positive impacts on workers' level of creativity in the workplace (measured by their employer's daily observation of workers' reported creative thoughts or problem-solving) that can last for up to two days.[8]

So what's the verdict here? Do bad moods lead to more creativity? Or is it good moods that do the trick?

Well, according to the psychologist Leonard Martin and his colleagues, it actually depends on the goal of the task at hand.

If the goal of whatever we're doing at the time is to do as much as we can, or for as long as we possibly can, then people in bad moods tend to put in much more effort and a lot more perseverance than those in good moods. Here, bad moods help keep us attuned to the task, while good moods send a signal to our brain that the job is now done, and that we can stop working. As a result, because people in bad moods tend to work much harder and be more productive than people in good moods in situations where they are told to do as much as they can, then bad moods can potentially lead to more creativity for the person.

On the contrary, if the goal of a task is not to do as much as we can but to carry on doing the task until we don't enjoy doing it any more, then it's the people in a better mood who put in more effort and are much more persistent at carrying out the task, and therefore more likely to produce something creative, than people in bad moods.[9]

So what's that in simple terms?

Well, happiness seems to spur more creativity – perhaps through more productivity – in more enjoyable jobs. In other words: 'If you still enjoy doing your job, then why stop?'[10] Of course, happiness will tell us to stop working if we're reminded that: 'Once you feel satisfied with your work, you should stop.' Hence the reason why happier people may put in less effort at work if the pre-programmed goal is for them to complete the task as far as they possibly can.

In other words, in these kinds of jobs, if we're already happy with the outcome, why should we carry on?

So, if this theory is true, then maybe – just maybe – painting was never really enjoyable to Vincent Van Gogh in the first place. And because he was always unhappy, maybe that's the reason why he was so successful at it.

But, of course, that's just conjecture.

So, there's certainly some evidence to suggest that happiness isn't just an output, but also an input, i.e., it can potentially increase our levels of creativity and productivity. But are there more reasons to believe that happiness is worth pursuing, not for its own sake but for benefits that are more objective and tangible than the ability to be creative and productive?

Are happier people more successful in life?

'Success is not the key to happiness. Happiness is the key to success.'

Albert Schweitzer

In 2005, three prominent American psychologists, Sonja Lyubomirsky of the University of California, Riverside, Ed Diener of the University of Illinois, and Laura King of the University of Missouri, published a review paper with one simple yet powerful conclusion: *happier people are more success-ful in life than unhappier ones.*[11]

That's definitely a big claim. The questions that remain are how and why?

Well, according to the three psychologists, there's over-whelming evidence from cross-sectional studies (i.e., looking at the general population at a given point in time), longitu-dinal studies (i.e., looking at the same individuals over time), and experimental studies (i.e., examining the cause and effect of something on an outcome among randomly-selected par-ticipants) suggesting that happier people tend to be more suc-cessful in three different domains in life compared to their less happy counterparts: work life, social relationships, and health.

With respect to being more successful at work, there's strong evidence to suggest that happiness correlates well with job per-formance. While this may be due to the positive link between good moods and levels of creativity, it may at the same time be due to the fact that happier workers tend not to be absent from work, not burn out quickly, and – unsurprisingly because they're happy individuals – not let their dissatisfaction be known to their employer through retaliatory behaviours.[12] In other words, happy workers are less likely to be fired from their jobs than unhappy workers for these behavioural reasons. The fact that happy people are also hard workers is also likely to be reflected in their incomes. So for example, in a longitudi-nal study by Ed Diener and his colleagues on the link between students' cheerfulness and their subsequent earnings, the more cheerful the students in the sample in the first year of university, the higher the probability that they would be earning higher incomes sixteen years later, holding other things constant.[13]

Happier people also tend to be more successful than oth-ers at finding someone to marry, on average. For example, in a longitudinal study tracking the same individuals through time in Australia, it was found that very happy people were 1.5 times more likely to be married at a later time period than those single people with average happiness[14] (although bear in mind that this may just be reflecting the anticipation effect of marriage already discussed in Chapter 6, in which people become happier in the year prior to marriage). A similar and yet perhaps more remarkable result was obtained in a study by psychologists Lee Anne Harker and Dacher Keltner of the University of California, Berkeley. By simply observing how happy the women in their sample looked in their college year book pictures, the two psychologists were able to demonstrate that, among those who eventually got married, the happier-looking women were more likely to still be married 30 years after their photos were taken, compared to those who were rated as slightly unhappier.[15] And this positive effect of happiness on the probability of remaining married 30 years later continued to be robust even when the women's physical attractiveness and willingness to please others (i.e., the social desirability factor) had been taken into account in the analysis. But it's not only in marriage that happier people fare better than less cheerful people; they are also more likely to receive emotional and tangible support from their friends over time.[16] In other words, happy people tend to be able to draw others to help and befriend them in their times of need.

Why is that? One simple (and rather obvious) reason: most people prefer to befriend someone who's happy than someone grumpy. Happy people, for instance, tend to smile 'Duchenne' or genuine smiles more often than unhappy people. Consequently, they tend to be thought of by others as friendly and open to social interaction, thus inviting others to become engaged in social relationships with them.[17] Befriending a happy person may also evoke positive feelings in the friends as well, which increases the likelihood that they will maintain the relationship.[18]

What about pro-social behaviours? Do happy people also behave more altruistically towards other people whom they may not even know? According to the American social psychologists Peggy Thoits of Indiana University and Lyndi Hewitt of Vanderbilt University, yes they do. Using an American longitudinal data set, they found that while doing voluntary work for the community makes people happy, happier people also tend to actively seek out voluntary work (although admittedly, it may also be the case that organisations that do voluntary work also prefer to employ happy people rather than grumpy people).[19]

How about the effects of happiness on health? Other than the study of nuns mentioned in Chapter 2, there's also physiological evidence that the experience of positive mood helps to lower the incidence of stroke six years later.[20] With respect to the short-term effects of happiness on health, it appears that experiences of positive moods correlate negatively with incidence of upper respiratory infection over a two-week period, as well as fewer emergency room and hospital visits on the next day.[21]

And that's not all. There's overwhelming evidence that happy people are significantly less likely to die from certain causes, including, among others, driving accidents.[22] Happy people also tend to survive for a significantly longer period following an illness. For example, studies have found that patients with end-stage kidney failure who rated themselves as happy with life overall were more likely to survive for up to four years longer than those who were less happy with their life; women who experienced a recurrence of breast cancer but also reported joy in their living were also more likely to survive for seven years longer than others; and those with spinal-cord injuries who were more satisfied with their lives were also more likely to survive for eleven years longer than other, less happy spinal injury patients.[23]

What these results are implying is that happy people tend to live longer. And given that happiness is highly correlated with a variety of favourable life outcomes (e.g., stable relationships, low accident and suicide rates, great emotional and physical support from close ones, and less stress), it should be no surprise, concluded Sonja Lyubomirsky, Ed Diener and Laura King, that happiness should also be positively correlated with longevity.

But are these results really due to unobserved personality traits? In other words, were those born with predispositions that keep them happy always destined to be more successful in life? If so, these favourable objective outcomes may not have much to do with happiness generated by external factors at all.

Well, perhaps some experimental evidence could shed some light on the cause and effect issue.

In controlled experiments in which good moods are typically induced by getting randomly-selected participants to watch short comedy film clips or listen to humorous stories, researchers have found that the induced short-term happiness is capable of leading people to behave in ways that parallel what we normally call success. This includes, for example, a study showing that male participants in whom positive moods had been induced were more likely to start engaging in social interaction with strangers of the opposite sex.[24] Induced happy moods also tend to lead participants to derive greater enjoyment from whatever activity they are instructed to perform by the experimenters, which seems to suggest that happy people are more likely than unhappy people to be more agreeable to almost everything they are asked or have to do.[25] They are also likely to judge other people less, and, immediately after having been induced to become happier, tend to start seeing the world in a positive light – so much so that, in job-hiring situations, interviewers who have been induced to feel happy tend to judge a job applicant whose qualifications are objectively ambiguous as favourable for the job, compared to interviewers who have been induced to experience negative emotions.[26] In other words, it may be a lot easier to get a job when being interviewed by a happy interviewing committee rather than an unhappy one.

And perhaps more amazingly, people who have been induced to feel happy tend to be observed to have increased levels of immunity.[27] It seems that happiness can really help decrease the chances of becoming ill in the future.

In summary, the case made by the three psychologists seems pretty convincing: happiness is not just a by-product of success; there's strong evidence to suggest that many successes in life are also a by-product of happiness as well.

In addition to this, the evidence that happiness can be thought of as an input as well as an output helps to explain why cause and effect needs to be sorted out whenever we're interpreting a relationship observed in an estimation of a simple happiness equation. We know from Chapters 4 and 5 that money can really make people happy. But, as clearly shown here, happier people – regardless of how they became happier in the first place – are also more likely than others to become more financially success-ful. The causality clearly runs in both directions.

And so maybe happiness isn't overrated after all. And the evi-dence presented above is sufficient reason why all of us should aim for exactly the same thing Jeremy Bentham wanted for his society all those years ago: the greatest happiness for the great-est number of people, better known as 'the greatest happiness principle'.

In other words, even though studies have found that hap-piness is often fleeting and that often we can't make someone happier without making someone else worse off (as in the case of the race for status), the evidence from 'happiness as input' studies provides yet another incentive for making the greatest happiness principle the main political objective for any society in the world. Just how we could ever achieve that, on the other hand, is still very much a contentious issue. I mean, how costly is it going to be to make everyone happier without making somebody feel worse off?

Good question. And yet it might not be as costly as one might think to make everybody happier. Ask Stanley Milgram.

It's a small world after all

Born in 1933 to a Jewish family in New York City, Stanley Milgram became known throughout the world for his controversial approach to psychology. A professor of social psychology at Yale University, he conducted hundreds of experiments, many of which produced results that shocked the world.[28] One in particular was an experiment on obedience in which Milgram observed that people would do almost anything – even administer electric shocks of 450 volts to someone they hardly knew – simply because somebody in authority was telling them to.[29]

And yet it was one of Milgram's less controversial experiments that really caught the attention of happiness researchers.

In the so-called 'small-world' experiment, Stanley Milgram began with the idea that any two people in the world can be linked even when they don't know each other directly. But linked to what degree, he didn't know. And so, in 1967, Milgram set out to test this theory by sending out small packets to randomly selected people in Omaha, Nebraska and Wichita, Kansas in the American Midwest.[30] Each of these packets contained a letter outlining the study's purpose, basic information about a target contact person, who was also chosen at random, in Boston (some 1,200 miles away on the US east coast), a roster on which each participant could write his or her own name before passing the packet forward, and business reply cards that were pre-addressed to Harvard where Milgram was working at the time. Each of the participants – starting in Omaha and Wichita – was asked by Milgram's letter to send the packet to a friend or acquaintance whom he or she thought would be most likely to know the target person, as well as sending one of the pre-paid business cards back to Milgram's office as a record. The procedure was simple, although there was one strict rule to which all participants had to conform: the packet could be sent only to a person whom the participant knew on a first-name basis. When and if the packet eventually arrived at the contact person in Boston, Milgram's research team could count how many times the packet had been passed from person to person.

So, on average, how many times did a packet have to be passed from person to person before it finally reached the contact in Boston? Approximately five or six (two and ten being the minimum and maximum path lengths). This led Milgram to conclude that any two people in America can be linked, on average, from the starter to the target in only five or six steps, which became popularly known as the 'six degrees of separation'.[31]

The scientific impact of Milgram's small-world experiment was dramatic. It led to a revolution in the science of networking and, consequently, an exploding number of researchers trying to apply the small-world problem to many other real-world scenarios. For instance, three economists, Sanjeev Goyal, Marco van der Leij and José Luis Moraga-González, published a study in the *Journal of Political Economy* reporting that the average distance between one economics author and another is roughly ten. In other words, author A may co-write a paper with author

B, who co-writes with author C and so on, and eventually a link between author A and author J can be established.[32]

But what's that got to do with the greatest happiness principle?

Well, consider this. If everybody in the world can be linked, and happiness itself is contagious among people within the same social network (in that one person's happiness is generally transmissible to another and then to another and so on), then maybe all we need to do in order to create a happy society is to focus on making a small number of people happier and then wait for that happiness to multiply, instead of trying to make every single individual in a society simultaneously happier.

But is that nothing more than wishful thinking?

Perhaps. But at least it's something that two American social scientists, James Fowler of the University of California, San Diego and Nicholas Christakis of Harvard University, are more than willing to find out.

The happiness bug

In their seminal study published in 2008 in the *British Medical Journal*,[33] Fowler and Christakis – the authors of *Connected*[34] – explored how happiness can be spread across a social network over time. Using a longitudinal data set taken from the Framingham Heart Study in America between 1983 and 2003, the two were able to show that the effect of one's happiness on other people's happiness is positive – people who are surrounded by many happy people and those who are central in the network are likely to become significantly happier in the future. More specifically, they found that we would become 25 per cent happier with our life if one of our friends who lives within a mile (1.6 kilometres) of us became happier with his or hers. (Nevertheless, the happiness of a friend who lives further away has no effect on the happiness of the respondent.)

Similar effects of 8 per cent are seen in co-resident spouses; the equivalent figures are 14 per cent for siblings who live within a mile of each other and 34 per cent for next-door neighbours. In other words, the magnitude of the happiness spread seems to depend more on frequent social contact (due to physical proximity) than deep social connections. However, they found no significant spill-over effect of happiness among co-workers, which seems to suggest that the social context might moderate the flow of happiness from one person to another. Finally, Fowler and Christakis concluded that these contagion effects of happiness get smaller with time and geographical distance, and that the potential mechanisms of the spread of happiness may include, among other things, happy people sharing their good fortune (for example, by being pragmatically helpful or by being financially generous), or changing their behaviours towards others (for example, by being nicer or less hostile), or merely exuding an emotion that is contagious.

This is a significant find: not only that all of us are interconnected in some way, but that there's now a possibility that our happiness can be transmitted from one person to another (although perhaps the contagion effect may not be as large or as durable as Jeremy Bentham – if he had known the result – would have liked it to be). Fowler and Christakis's findings have since been strengthened by a newly released study on spousal correlation in happiness in the UK: an increase in one spouse's happiness in the past has been found to have a positive and significant effect on the other spouse's happiness today. Additionally, a spouse whose happiness has just been increased by the other spouse's happiness is likely to remain in the marriage for a longer period of time.[35]

It might be useful at this point to project what might happen if Fowler and Christakis's results could be combined with

Milgram's findings that every person in the world is interlinked. Provided that Fowler and Christakis's findings hold generally, I could expect to become 25 per cent happier, on average, from one of my friends who lives in close proximity to me – let's call him Sam – becoming happier. I could also expect my happiness to have yet another spill-over effect on the happiness of my other friends. For example, another one of my friends – let's call her Debbie – may get a 25 per cent share of the 25 per cent hit in happiness I have recently experienced from Sam becoming happier, even if Sam may not know Debbie directly. According to Fowler and Christakis, this contagion effect of one's happiness extends up to three degrees of separation, so my happiness can affect the happiness of the friends of my friends' friends.

Imagine, then, as a stylised example, that other than Sam and Debbie I also have several other friends living in close proximity to me but who don't know each other directly. So, as well as Sam who I know from college and Debbie who I know from school, I also know Mark who lives next door to me, Robert who I often go hiking with on the weekends, and Richard who I play tennis with every Tuesday night. All of these friends will also benefit from me becoming 25 per cent happier because Sam became happier with his life. Now imagine that each of them also has friends of his or her own. What may be the result of this? A potential epidemic of a good kind.

In other words, there's a wider benefit to becoming happy: there's a positive externality effect of our happiness on other people's happiness. We can make other people happier just by being happy ourselves. And if we can hold on to our happiness long enough for it to spread, then perhaps Jeremy Bentham's idea of an egalitarian society in terms of happiness may not be such an abstract idea any more.

But could there be a contagion effect for *unhappiness*, too? Can unhappiness, like happiness, spread like wildfire? You bet.

While research on the contagion effect of happiness is relatively new, psychologists have actually been studying the contagion effects of stress and strain across two individuals from as early as the 1980s. For example, the American psychologist Niall Bolger of Columbia University and his colleagues have published several studies reporting evidence that stress experienced by a spouse at work often raises the level of stress experienced by the other spouse at home,[36] which contributes to a notable increase in the incidence of negative moods and stress-related health problems not only for those in full-time employment but also for those at home.[37] A similar result is obtained in other relationships; in a recent study by myself and Anna Vignoles, a professor of economics of education at the University of London, bad moods experienced by parents in the previous year were associated with a significantly lower level of their children's happiness this year. In other words, a stressed parent – whether it's a mum or a dad – can lead to a large drop in terms of happiness for their children, which could potentially impact on how they perform at school and, later, in life.[38]

You might be wondering at this point: 'Are you suggesting, then, that happiness is the be-all and end-all?' No, would be my answer. The evidence suggests only that happy people tend to live longer and healthier. They tend to be more productive, sometimes creative, and are able to maintain good relationships with other people for a much longer period of time compared to someone who is less happy. It doesn't mean, however, that happy people will succeed in every single domain of life, considering that negative feelings can sometimes be useful in situations where critical thinking and error-checking are required.[39] And more significantly, as pointed out by Raymond Belliotti, to live a meaningful life is in itself a virtue, and should therefore never be discouraged or discounted.

All I'm suggesting is that if being healthier, living longer, being more productive and creative at work, and having a good social life and happier friends surrounding you happen to be your goals in life, then perhaps happiness itself should never be forsaken, either.

One question of interest here is: If we want society as a whole to become happier, how can we avoid making somebody else feel worse off in the process of making us feel better off? We know that the individual pursuit of status doesn't help. We can try to encourage people to spend more time with their family and friends, which is, according to the overwhelming evidence in the science of happiness, the kind of experience that's both welfare-increasing for the individual and not welfare-decreasing for others (unless you're the employer and the individual happens to be missing work over it). However, as long as people's preferences are still tied up with the need to keep up with the Joneses, then these words of advice are likely to fall on deaf ears.

So what do we do? Perhaps some government interventions are needed to steer all of us towards greater happiness without making anybody feel worse off in return. But is that a good thing, having a paternalistic authority telling us what to do if we want to be happier? Can't we just use the information provided by the findings from the psychology and economics of happiness as a guide and attempt to carry it out ourselves? How successful would that be? And, in relation to Belliotti's comments about the pursuit of a meaningful life but not happiness itself, could there be experiences that are both meaningful and, at the same time, generating us plenty of happiness in return? Put simply, can we have it all? Can we have our cake and eat it too?

CHAPTER 10

WHO GETS TO DECIDE?

Jigme Singye Wangchuk was no average ruler. Crowned the youngest-ever King of Bhutan (a small country in South Asia, located at the eastern end of the Himalaya mountains) at the age of eighteen in 1974, he had a vision from the start to improve his country in ways that may seem strange or unfeasible to anyone living in the Western world. But during his 31-year reign, he almost single-handedly introduced free health and educational services aimed at covering *everyone* in his country,[1] a feat so impressive that many affluent countries in the West couldn't even begin to fathom how it could be done. Roads and bridges seemed to emerge out of nowhere to reach the most remote parts of the rugged terrain of Bhutan. More notably, Bhutanese life expectancy also improved drastically during his kingship from 38 years to 66 years. Household incomes, however, remained among the lowest in the world at around $4,000 per person per annum.

According to Stefan Priesner, a United Nations Development Programme officer in Bhutan, the success (or failure – it depends on whether you're looking at the vast improvement in the social infrastructure or the slow economic growth during the 31 years) of Bhutan's development can be attributed largely to the king's powerful vision: to have people's happiness at the very heart of the country's development plan.[2] His concept of 'Gross National Happiness' (GNH) consists of the promotion of equitable and sustainable socio-economic development, preservation and promotion of cultural values, conservation of the natural environment, and establishment of good governance.[3] To achieve these, the Royal Bhutanese government has introduced policies that range from limiting the number of TV channels (and banning programmes like wrestling matches and MTV) and restricting advertising in general on the grounds that it can lead to higher expectation for individuals, to banning plastic bags and tobacco because they could potentially harm the environment and personal health and therefore make people less happy.[4]

While these radical policies have been adopted successfully in Bhutan in the sense that nobody in the country had anything bad to say about them when they were first introduced (perhaps partly because it's a country that was ruled by an absolute monarch until 2008), the question is whether they could also be successfully implemented by other governments in the world, like those of Britain and America, and if they can really promise a higher and sustainable level of happiness for all of us.

* * *

I met Paul Frijters for the first time during one of my summer visits to Thailand in 2007. A professor of economics at Queensland University of Technology in Australia (and, in 2009, named Best Australian Economist under the age of 40 by the Australian Economic Society), Paul stood out from the crowd like a sore thumb, with his cowboy hat and plain white shirt. I went to introduce myself, half hoping that he'd be one of the friendly ones there. Luckily, he was, and we ended up getting on like a house on fire.

We were attending a conference on happiness and public policies at the United Nations Development Programme (UNDP) regional centre in Bangkok. The aim of the conference, organised by the Thai government and the UNDP, was to promote the idea that happiness should be one of the main objectives in all public policies in Thailand and elsewhere in the world. Paul was there as one of the invited keynote speakers.

While waiting for his scheduled slot, Paul turned to me and asked: 'Nick, am I allowed to say *anything* here?' The question took me by surprise, but I replied 'Yes' anyway. There was no reason to imagine that he could say anything to offend anyone in here. Half an hour later, Paul took to the stage in front of the audience of 500, which included the deputy prime minister of Thailand and the ex-prime minister of Bhutan.

'It's good to see you all here today,' he began. 'Ten years ago, happiness economics was in the dog house. Nobody wanted to know what we were doing, everyone always mistrusted the value of looking at how people felt about their lives, and most economists simply took it as a valid assumption that only economic growth is important. Many people in this room have waited a long time for happiness to be taken seriously by the rest of the world and it's nice to share this conference with you. I feel myself among friends.

'However, friends have to tell each other the truth, even if it's uncomfortable.' Paul's face had turned serious now. 'The video you showed us at the beginning of the conference showed a village with poor individuals who were supposedly rich in social contacts and happy. The message of the video was that economic growth would lead these villagers into losing those networks, becoming obsessed with status and competition, and thus losing their happiness.

'Yet I ask who is making these recommendations. Are the people who don't want others to get richer giving up their own wealth? In that regard I notice a whole room full today of very well-dressed people, with nice cars outside, laptops in front of them, staying in posh hotels and regularly flying all over the world. You ask villagers to do something you do not do yourself. If we ourselves chase money, knowing full well that we do this mainly because of status considerations, surely we cannot deny the same to these villagers.

'Also, when I reflect on how local social networks get destroyed, it's simply not true that it's internationalisation and global competition that does this. You as the Thai government do this by building schools, hospitals and roads in the countryside. It's those schools and hospitals that replace the services of the grandmother or the local healer and that thus take away the economic reason for local networks. It's the road to the village that allows the villagers to escape the local social network and come to the city. It's not international capital that builds that road, school or hospital. You as the Thai government do it and you do it because you partially want to alleviate poverty. Hence if we ask the question what makes people status-oriented and destroys local social ties, we need not look at research or at others. We need only to look inside ourselves for the answers.'

Paul later told me that this was a case of *de bittere waarheid*: the brutal truth. Someone's got to say it. And even though I was apprehensive of what the Thai government officials might be thinking about his speech, in hindsight I think Paul was right to say what he said.

And, yes, someone's got to hear it, too.

Trust me – I'm a happiness expert

Paul's speech at the Thai conference hits the nail on the head by prompting us to think not only about *what* makes us happy, but also *who* has the right to decide on what should make us happy.

What about us? Shouldn't we be the ones who get to decide what's good for our own well-being and what's not? The evidence presented in this book has suggested otherwise: we have learnt from Chapter 1 (and Chapter 8 when the focusing illusion was the topic of discussion) that most of us aren't that great at predicting accurately our emotional reactions to many experiences in our lives. When we think about how happy we'll be after an event, especially one that's novel to us, we tend to misallocate our attention towards the most salient features of the experience in question – for example, people tend to mispredict that disabled people must be very unhappy with their lives, and that parents must be significantly happier than non-parents. While some of these mispredictions are perhaps justifiable on the grounds that the chosen experiences are meaningful (even though spending time with kids doesn't make us significantly happier on average, it *is* fulfilling), other mispredictions can potentially lead to a socially wasteful outcome.

Take the misprediction about the true impact of money on our happiness. Because of our intrinsic need to be ranked higher than other people in our reference group, the pursuit of greater incomes can lead to more time spent commuting to and from work and less time spent doing activities with friends and family (Chapter 3). And since the pursuit of rank or 'keeping up with the Joneses' is a zero-sum game (i.e., for every winner there's also a loser), and the evidence is that we tend not to adapt completely to commuting (Chapter 6), such a misprediction can result in a prolonged reduction in aggregate well-being for the nation as a whole.

In short, research on happiness seems to call for some kind of government intervention in order to correct for the more harmful consequences of our mispredictions on what makes us happy in the long run. The question is: How much intervention should there be? This takes us to the other extreme of the 'who gets to decide' scale. If we're so dreadful at choosing what's right and wrong for ourselves, then maybe we should just leave it to the government to guide us to making better choices at both individual and societal levels.

One of the main advocates of government interventions is the English economist Richard Layard of the London School of Economics. He published a study in 2006 outlining potential policy implications based on the evidence found in the happiness research.[5]

For example, one of the common findings in the happiness literature is that people care a great deal about relative status. In other words, there's evidence to suggest that other people's incomes have a negative effect upon our well-being, holding our income constant. To correct for this negative externality effect, Layard proposes that a higher tax rate on income should be imposed on the labour force. His reasoning is simple: if the existing tax system doesn't do enough to discourage people from working too hard in order to keep up with the Joneses, then a higher tax rate – one that will reduce work effort to a level where the socially wasteful incentive to raise our relative income has been fully offset – should be implemented. Hence, a higher tax rate will act as a stabiliser on our intrinsic yet collectively fruitless need to pursue higher status.

Focusing illusion may also induce people to overestimate how long the extra happiness from extra material goods will last. As indicated in Chapter 6, because a prospective pay rise seems much more salient than a two-hour commute, people may overestimate how long the extra happiness from a pay rise will last. At the same time, they may also underestimate how long it will take them to completely adapt to the unhappiness brought about by the commute. And because of this misprediction, many will choose to endure a long commute in return for more money in the bank, believing that they will be fully compensated for it (which, in many cases, they won't).[6] In situations such as these, the government might decide to increase the price of public transport for those doing long commutes, thus raising the opportunity cost of taking a better-paid job but one that's nevertheless far from home.

Libertarian paternalism

To many, Layard's approach of so-called 'happiness policies', such as his proposition of corrective taxation on the pursuit of status, is perhaps a little too paternalistic.[7] It's like our parents telling us to floss after brushing or to always finish our greens. But although we may not like the idea of it, surely we'll benefit from it in the long run? Given that we aren't such a perfect judge of what's good for us anyway, why should we care when the ends seem to justify the means?

One natural argument against Layard's idea of 'hard' paternalism, in which some kinds of bands and mandates are imposed on the population, is that people still care a great deal about their freedom of choice. In a study that explores the role of freedom on people's happiness, the Dutch sociologist Ruut Veenhoven has been able to show that, despite the fact that we don't always make correct choices, the opportunity to choose whether to become richer or not – i.e. economic freedom – in the absence of restriction correlates positively and significantly with people's well-being for many countries in the West.[8] What this implies is that, given the option between a chance to choose and make a mistake and having no choice at all but knowing the outcome will always be good, the majority of people would still prefer to have the choice. Perhaps that's just human nature: a freedom to choose (or at least, the perception that there's a freedom to choose) means that we have, to an extent, some power or control over the way we want our life to turn out.

So it might be hard for any government to try to convince its people that higher taxes can make them happy. But maybe there's a gentler approach to policy-making that the government could take in order to guide its citizens to a better, happier life. That approach, introduced and popularised by Richard Thaler and Cass Sunstein's *Nudge*,[9] is 'libertarian paternalism'.

An oxymoron, at least on the face of it, libertarian paternalism relies on the same principles of 'corrective' policy as Layard's hard paternalism, but with a slight twist. Equipped with the knowledge that people's rationality is bounded by the information they have at the time of making the decision, it may be possible for the state to design the kind of public policy that would not only steer people away from making bad decisions, but also do it in a way that respects their freedom of choice.[10]

For instance, a series of studies by psychologists Daniel Kahneman and Amos Tversky has shown that the majority of people respond not only to incentives but also to subtle suggestive instructions. According to the two scholars, people tend to make inconsistent decisions, depending on whether the scenario is framed to them as losses or gains.[11] And because 'a win doesn't feel as good as a loss feels bad' (see 'loss aversion' described in Chapter 7), it's possible for the government to use this to its advantage and alter people's preferences for the better without any coercion involved. So, for example, individuals have been shown to evaluate a new economic programme more favourably when it's described as resulting in a '95 per cent employment rate' than when described as resulting in a '5 per cent unemployment rate'[12] – even though both options are exactly the same. This so-called 'framing effect' has also been shown to be strong enough to influence not only people's stated preferences, but also their actual behaviours. Psychology professors Beth Meyerowitz of the University of Southern

California and Shelly Chaiken of New York University discovered that women who were exposed to loss-framed information about breast cancer – i.e., *not* performing a breast examination *decreases* the chance of finding a treatable tumour – were more likely to engage in examinations than women who were exposed to gain-framed information: performing a breast examination increases the chance of finding a treatable tumour.[13]

Additionally, consistent with the findings on framing effects, a recent study by me and my colleagues, Michalis Drouvelis of the University of York and Robert Metcalfe of Oxford University, has shown that we can induce people to behave even more altruistically than their normal selves just by getting them to play a word search game – a word game that requires the player to find and mark all the words hidden in a grid. What we found is that individuals who had been primed to think cooperatively at the start of the experiment (we did this by getting our participants to do a word search game filled with hidden words like *community*, *team work*, and *sharing*) were more likely to contribute more of their own money to a community project – an act that benefits *everyone* in the community in the long run – than those who had been neutrally primed, who were asked to play a word search game filled with hidden words like *lamp*, *umbrella*, and *gasoline*.[14] In other words, just getting people to think cooperatively makes them behave cooperatively – even when their own money is at stake. The results are consistent with studies in psychology finding that people who have been primed with words associated with elderly stereotypes like *grey*, *old*, and *withdraw* tend to walk from one end of a corridor to the other at a much slower pace than those who have been primed with neutral words.[15]

What's even more surprising is that we also find that almost all of the participants who were primed with cooperative words didn't even suspect that they had been manipulated to think cooperatively at all. More importantly, the cooperatively-primed individuals reported to be happier afterwards with the community outcomes than those who were primed with neutral words.

Another cognitive bias that has been studied extensively in the libertarian paternalism literature is the 'status quo bias': people's tendency not to deviate from their current choice or their established behaviour unless the incentive to change is compelling.[16] This type of cognitive bias can be illustrated easily – and has been done so regularly on the American TV game show *Let's Make a Deal*, which was hosted by Monty Hall from the 1960s to the early 1990s.

In *Let's Make a Deal*, the participants are faced with the following dilemma. First, the host presents a contestant with the choice of three doors. The host then tells the contestant that behind one door there's a car, which the contestant can win. Behind the other two doors, however, are goats. The contestant is then told to pick a door that he or she thinks has a car behind it. Once a door is picked, the host – *who knows what's behind each of the three doors* – opens another door that he knows has a goat behind it. He then tells the contestant: 'Now that there are two doors left – hence, a probability of 50 per cent that a car will be behind one of these doors – I'm going to give you one more chance to switch from the door you picked in the beginning to the other one. Would you switch?'[17]

Now, if you're like most contestants in *Let's Make a Deal*, the chances are that you'll choose not to switch to the other door: you'll stick with the door you picked right from the start. And like most contestants, you'd be facing a probability of 1/3 of winning the car, on average. The correct decision, however, would always be to switch door; if you did, then on average you'd be facing a probability of 2/3 of winning the car.

'Wait a minute,' you'd probably object. 'Isn't the probability of winning 50 per cent (i.e. 1/2), no matter whether I switch or stick to my original choice?'

Not quite.

In this so-called 'Monty Hall problem', our tendency to strongly favour the status quo can be explained by two cognitive biases. The first is that we tend to let our emotions or intuitions overrule reason – whether it's logical or statistical. It might not happen to everyone, but many people stumble when it comes to doing quick maths in their head. However, assuming we could readily do so, then it would be fairly easy for us to come up with the following solution to the Monty Hall problem when faced with it for the first time. Given three doors to choose from in the beginning, it's simple to see that there's a 1/3 chance of us picking the correct door with a car behind it. Once a door is chosen at random and the host has *non-randomly* opened a door with a goat staring at us, two doors are left: the one we picked at the beginning of the game and the other the remaining unpicked door.

Our immediate intuition will tell us that there's now a 50 per cent chance of winning the car, so why switch? Nevertheless, a little more reasoning suggests that the host's decision to *always* open one of the doors with a goat behind it doesn't change the original probability of us picking the correct door from the start: the door we picked will still have a 1/3 probability of winning the car, while the other two hold a 2/3 probability of having a car behind them. Since the now opened door (the one with the goat behind it) clearly has a zero probability of being the correct door, all of the 2/3 probability now lies with the remaining unopened door. So, since a 2/3 chance is higher than a 1/3 chance, it becomes a no-brainer that we should always switch door.[18]

But the interesting question here is why, when we're under the mistaken assumption that it's 50–50 that the car is behind either one of the two remaining doors, do most of us (rather than 50 per cent of us) decide not to switch, when switching itself doesn't seem to bear any obvious cost to us?

The second cognitive bias is a combination of two related effects: the endowment effect[19] – our tendency to value something more when its property has been established – and cognitive dissonance – the uncomfortable feelings caused by holding two contradictory beliefs simultaneously ('I know smoking is bad for my health, but it's so addictive!'), which lead individuals to try to reduce this dissonance by altering their attitudes to favour their original decisions ('Smoking may be bad for some, but it helps to reduce weight; so if I stop smoking, I'll gain weight, which is bad for me.').[20] Faced with two *seemingly* 50–50 choices, most people believe that they will regret it more if they switch and make a mistake than if they don't switch and make a mistake. In other words, people tend to believe that *forgone gains are less painful than perceived losses*, which is a typical implication of the endowment effect.[21] Additionally, given that each one of us tends to seek for a way that will allow us to avoid having to hold two conflicting ideas simultaneously in our head ('What do I do? The car could be behind either one of these doors!'), the availability of an alternative choice – one that we have already rejected from the very start – has the ability to skew our preferences towards retaining our original choice in a big way.

Why?

Well, given the alternative of the remaining unopened door, we tell ourselves that we never wanted it anyway, thereby sparing ourselves the painfully dissonant thought that we made the wrong decision right from the beginning.[22]

These are just a few examples of findings from psychology and behavioural economics that soft-paternalistic policy could be based upon, having the ability to change people's preferences and behaviours without infringing too much on their freedom of choice. Some have already been implemented to correct certain irrational behaviours, although not always with the sole aim of maximising people's happiness. So, for example, we know from the evidence in the economics of happiness literature that people care about their relative income *per se*. Therefore, one implication of this finding is that people will tend to save relatively little early in their lives, partly because income is often spent on goods that signal status such as cars or plasma TVs. And since saving requires a degree of self-control, most individuals have been found to lack the will-power to maintain that high level of commitment to save all the time. Additionally, most people who save too little early in their life tend to procrastinate and think that whatever they will be doing later won't be as important as what they are doing now. The outcome of these cognitive biases – relative income effect, self-control problem, and procrastination – is that consumption will not be smoothed out over the life cycle, and people will later find themselves with little savings when the time comes to retire.

So what do we do? How do we encourage higher saving rates among low-saving households without forcing them to do so?

In a seminal study, the economists Richard Thaler and Shlomo Benartzi of the University of California, Los Angeles found that when workers in a firm were enrolled into a saving programme called Save More Tomorrow™, which commits people in advance to allocating a portion of their future incomes towards retirement savings but with an opportunity to opt out should they wish, rather than giving them a free choice right from the start of whether to opt in to a high-saving-rate programme, the result was a significant increase in the workers' average saving rate from 3.5 per cent to 13.6 per cent over the course of under four years.[23] More surprisingly, the enrolment didn't lead to a lot of fuss from the workers who joined the programme; out of everyone who joined, 80 per cent remained in the programme through the fourth pay rise.

What Thaler and Benartzi did was subtle, but extremely effective. Equipped with the knowledge that people tend to suffer from status quo bias – the tendency to retain original choices unless the incentive to change is compelling – they knew that, after joining the Save More Tomorrow™ programme, the majority of individuals were less likely to drop out from it, partly because of the endowment effect and partly because of cognitive dissonance. And it's not that they were being told what to do (they could leave the programme whenever they liked), so their freedom of choice remained intact.

Status quo bias has also been considered as an effective strategy to boost the rate of organ donation in countries where the donation rate is extremely low. In a remarkable study by Eric Johnson and Daniel Goldstein, organ donation rates were found to be substantially higher in countries that operate opt-out ('If you *don't* want to donate your organs, please tick the box') rather than opt-in schemes ('If you *do* want to donate your organs, please tick the box').[24] For instance, in countries like Austria, Belgium and France where the opt-out scheme is used, the rates of organ donation are close to 100 per cent. By contrast, less than 20 per cent of people are registered organ donors in Denmark, the UK and Germany, where the opt-in scheme is implemented.[25]

Hence, as far as we can tell, soft paternalism is not only effective, but also cost-friendly. Some might even say scary, considering how much people's attitudes and behaviours can be affected by simple and subtle manipulations.

And yet, in principle, when combined with the findings from happiness research, it may be possible for governments to apply the same libertarian paternalistic philosophy to help boost people's psychological well-being in a long-lasting and perhaps meaningful way. For instance, if we go back to the study by Mathew White and Paul Dolan assessing the richness of daily activities (see the end of Chapter 8) we find that, while time spent with children isn't always pleasurable but is nevertheless meaningful, some activities are actually rich in both happiness and meaningfulness.[26] These activities include, but are not limited to, volunteering, exercising, praying/meditating, reading/using the internet, socialising, and outdoor activities. By contrast, pleasurable activities such as watching TV and eating rank relatively low in terms of meaningfulness. So, given that the government is aware that the majority of its citizens are suffering from a weak will with respect to watching TV and over-eating (pleasurable activities, but not so rewarding), then it may choose to pursue a policy that makes activities such as volunteering or outdoor exercise much more attractive in comparison.

Happiness research as a means to improve the political process

So far in this book, I've been talking about the nature of happiness, how it's often fleeting, relative, and yet contagious, and that if we could somehow maintain some of it on a daily basis, how beneficial it would be to our lives. But ultimately, perhaps, it's an individual choice whether or not to become happier – not a mandate. With this in mind, what if some of us actually choose to engage in activities that are not pleasurable but are nevertheless rewarding, not because we have made a systematic mistake, but simply because our goal in life is not the pursuit of happiness but the pursuit of meaning? How could the government possibly distinguish between these two groups of individuals – one that is behaving irrationally, the other that chooses not to pursue happiness right from the start – and decide whether an intervention is required or even desirable?

So, yes, I may not be very happy every day. Yes, it may be a pain raising my children and doing the kind of work I do. And yes, I'm aware that happy people are more likely to be successful in different areas of life compared to unhappy people. And, yes, I'm also aware that there's this thing called focusing illusion that explains how people tend to exaggerate the importance of just about anything while they're thinking about it. But I wouldn't have it any other way. And there's no reason for anyone to force me to be happy, either.

If that's the case, then what's the good of happiness research in the bigger scheme of things, when there are so many potential problems and uncertainties associated with the maximisation of people's happiness?

According to economists Bruno Frey and Alois Stutzer, findings from happiness research should be used only to provide insights, which can then be introduced into the political discussion process, rather than as a reason for the state to come up with specific policy interventions.[27] The two scholars argue that the political objective of creating public policy to maximise people's happiness is a flawed philosophy for several reasons. First, there's a principal–agent problem, whereby what the people (the *principal*) want and what the government (the *agent* hired by the principal) wants may not be the same. In other words, it's unlikely to be the case that any government in the world is made up of purely benevolent politicians wanting to make the population as happy as possible. Rather, politicians also have their own objectives when it comes to designing public policy – that is, the probability that it will lead to them being re-elected.

The second reason, somewhat related to the first, is that if the aim to maximise people's happiness becomes a political objective, then an indicator of happiness has to be created to either replace or complement the existing well-being indicators such as GDP or Human Development Index (HDI). This isn't necessarily a bad thing. However, having a new indicator of happiness implies that the government may manipulate it to suit its goals. Because happiness is subjective by nature, it's easier for a bad government to influence it using policies that give the people immediate pleasures without considering how this may affect their future well-being – for example, giving out loans with low interest rates to people with poor credit ratings, thereby raising their immediate happiness, but without warning them about the potential hazards of conspicuous consumption, which could adversely affect their happiness in the future. Additionally, citizens themselves may have an incentive to misrepresent their happiness levels strategically in order to influence government policy in their favour.

For these reasons, Frey and Stutzer argue that insights from happiness research should be used only to improve the nature of the political process, which is an entirely different objective from that of maximising the nation's happiness. The best we can hope for is that happiness research will enable individuals to become better at developing the idea of what constitutes a good life, both individually and collectively. And in countries where democracy is a right, the findings from happiness research will then have to prove themselves in political competition and in the discourse among citizens, and between citizens and politicians. And only when the people agree that they do need to take suggestions from libertarian paternalists, perhaps because they have come to realise that their unhappiness is caused by their lack of self-control and procrastination, then – and only then – an implementation of a policy aimed at improving people's happiness will be morally justified.

* * *

The debate on whether the state should have any role in its population's happiness goes on.[28] Nevertheless, one thing is clear. Never before has any world leader taken much interest in this particular issue; that is, until now. Commissioned by French president Nicolas Sarkozy, the 2009 Stiglitz–Sen–Fitoussi report on the measurement of economic performance and social progress proposes a shift in the focus of statistics, from purely economic indicators like GDP or inflation to well-being and sustainability indicators like happiness and life satisfaction.[29] David Cameron, the UK's Conservative prime minister, is also a big fan of happiness and even said in a pre-election speech in February 2010 that, if elected, he would make libertarian paternalism one of the party's top priorities to nudge people towards happiness.[30] Now that he has reached Number Ten, it remains to be seen what he will achieve in this area.

So are we moving in the right direction? What would the face of politics be like if happiness really became one of the main objective goals for governments? Would we fall into the trap that Frey and Stutzer warned us of? Or would we arise from it fresher and, more importantly, happier than ever before?

Now that it's fashionable for politicians to try to put people's happiness before almost everything else, we may not have to wait long to find out.

CHAPTER 11

AND THE FUNNY THING IS?

This book started with several 'what if' questions, but one perhaps stood out the most. What if we can, with some degree of accuracy, measure and study people's emotional reactions to different life events, and then write a complete guidebook about the impact on our well-being of each one of them? How would we react to that?

Well, at first, we'd probably feel somewhat let down by the results; many findings from happiness research aren't exactly what we expected them to be. For instance, the things we tend to believe to be synonymous with happiness – having children and becoming rich are two primary examples – often don't live up to our expectations. Time heals but not always completely, depending on the kind of wound, while happiness itself is often transitory and requires a lot of commitment to maintain it. We also find that whatever we may be thinking about at the time, more often than not we'll exaggerate the value that it brings. What about the role of the state? Can the government help guide us towards happiness? Yes, but not without controversy and risk involved.

But there's a more positive side to all this. Although time doesn't completely heal all wounds – especially unemployment – we appear to adapt completely and quickly to marital breakdown and the death of our loved ones. Misery loves company, and so sometimes it may be good to share our unfortunate experiences with other people who are experiencing the same event. Happiness is also contagious, which means that one person's happiness has the potential to spread to everyone in close proximity to him or her. And even if money doesn't buy us as much happiness as we thought it would, time spent with friends, family and neighbours does. Finally, there's now a clear, objective goal to becoming happier, as the feeling of happiness can potentially lead us to be more creative, productive, successful in social situations, and healthier in the long run.

There may also be a feeling of hope that, with the availability of happiness data, we can now do so many things that were either impossible to do or not done very well previously. This includes, for example, using happiness data to value non-marketable goods like friendships, marriage, children, health, clean air, and maybe some day, even love. These values can then be used to decide how much money may be needed to compensate tort victims in court. They may even tell us exactly how much resources should be directed towards improving healthcare and the environment – two of the things that are, by definition, difficult to place monetary values on – simply by estimating how much health and environment matter to our happiness.[1] We can even use these values to help with our daily decision-making processes. For example, if the increase in happiness from a pay rise that comes from moving to a new job doesn't compensate for the loss in happiness from having to do a long commute, then maybe it's not worth the move after all.

Data on happiness can also be used to test abstract theories – economic or otherwise – that we haven't been able to test before. Without them, we would probably never have found out whether or not people habituate (or adapt) completely to marriage or the death of loved ones. And so, in principle, we may also be able to use them to test, for instance, whether parents are very good at predicting their children's happiness; whether people care about any other kind of ranking other than income;

or even whether terrorism in one country affects the well-being of people living in other countries.[2]

* * *

So, what are the next big steps in happiness research? In my opinion, there are two steps to be taken at present. The first is to try to find further objective evidence to support the notion that subjective well-being is worth recording and analysing at the national level. Although the statistical links between physiological indicators and self-reported happiness scores described in Chapter 2 essentially suggest that the latter are not random numbers, one might argue, for instance, that these indicators are not themselves unambiguous proxies of true human happiness or unhappiness. Without further confirmation that these self-reported well-being answers really – and I mean *really* – measure what every nation in the world intrinsically wants to monitor, i.e. the welfare of its people, then there will always be doubt, especially among hard-core economists who refuse to budge on the idea, about whether happiness data will mean anything useful outside epidemiological and medical literature.

To make one of the first passes at this problem, Andrew Oswald and Steve Wu from Hamilton College in the US have recently provided evidence that self-rated happiness answers are not only correlated in the expected directions with various biological indicators at the individual level, but also with the way people in the US choose where they want to live. Their idea is pretty simple: if data on happiness is a truly valid measure of people's inner well-being, then average happiness will be high in areas that have characteristics that human beings find objectively pleasant, and low in areas with characteristics that human beings find objectively unpleasant.

Published in the early 2010 issue of *Science*, Oswald and Wu's study found average happiness to be high in places where the objective index of state-by-state quality of life is better – quality of life normally being calculated and published in the form of house prices in various magazines in the US. (A combination of more sunshine, low student–teacher ratio, better air quality, low commuting time, low state and local taxes, high state and local expenditures on higher education, public welfare, highways and corrections, cost of living, etc., is assumed to drive up house prices, which can then be used as a revealed signal of higher quality of life.[3]) According to their published study, the top three happiest places to live in the US are 1) Louisiana,[4] 2) Hawaii, and 3) Florida; and the top three unhappiest states to live in are 1) New York, 2) Michigan, and 3) New Jersey. And according to the published ranking of state-by-state quality of life, out of the 50 calculated states, Louisiana ranks number 8, Hawaii number 38, and Florida number 10; while New York ranks 50, Michigan 49, and New Jersey 47. In sum, the happiness responses seem to be positively and fairly strongly correlated with places that many Americans believe to be better to live in.

The second next big step may see economists working more closely with the world's best medics and epidemiologists to create a new, objective measure of human happiness that can be used at the national level. This idea is initiated from a study published in the *Journal of Health Economics* in 2008, presenting a remarkable relationship between self-rated happiness and average country-by-country hypertension levels (hypertension defined as having a systolic blood pressure of 140 mmHg or above and/or a diastolic blood pressure of 90 mmHg or above): the happier the nation, the lower the risk of hypertension for the people in that country.[5] This bears close resemblance to the famous Whitehall study of British civil servants conducted by epidemiologists Andrew Steptoe of University College London and Jane Wardle of the Institute of Psychiatry in London, in which they found a negative and statistically important correlation between self-reported well-being and the cortisol level in the respondent's saliva.[6] (Cortisol is usually referred to in the medical field as the 'stress hormone', and is produced within our adrenal gland.)

Given the stunning correlations between happiness data and the different measures of biomarkers, it doesn't seem such a crazy proposal for countries around the world to start collecting data on blood pressure and cortisol levels as reasonable proxies for the well-being of their populations. This is because, while hard-core economists may still frown upon using happiness data to measure a nation's progress simply because they are subjective, it would be harder for them to use the same argument against objective and medically-accepted biomarker measures in the construction of a national well-being index, which, according to the Stiglitz–Sen–Fitoussi committee, would eventually be used to replace the simple GDP index adopted by governments in the 20th century.

* * *

Research on happiness has definitely helped answer many of the questions I had about what constitutes a good life, and so I have always taken pride in the findings. But it was only recently that I decided to tell one of my grandmothers in Thailand about what I do for a living, believing that she would be impressed beyond belief. And so, during one of my visits there, I told her that money makes people happy, but often not as much as we think. I told her that people habituate to good things, but also adapt to adverse events in their lives. I even told her one of the most advanced findings to date in the happiness literature: that we tend to exaggerate the importance of anything while we're thinking about it.

My grandmother – a devout Buddhist, an ex-farmer with no formal education, 90 years of age, who looks like Yoda from *Star Wars* every time she smiles – leaned closer and whispered to me: 'Tell me something I don't already know.'

And the funny thing is? She's absolutely spot-on.

The enlightened prince

The son of King Shuddodana and Queen Mahamaya who used to rule a small kingdom that is now southern Nepal, Prince Siddhartha Gautama had been born to a life of privilege. But only seven days after his birth in 483 BC, his mother sadly died. Concerned for his son's future, King Shuddodana had asked a well known fortune-teller, Asita, to predict Siddhartha's future. Asita foresaw two different possibilities for Siddhartha's life. The first was that Siddhartha would become the greatest king who had ever lived, an emperor who would rule all the lands. The second possibility was that he would become a great sage and saviour of humanity. And in doing so, he would leave the comfortable life of the palace and live the life of a hermit:

He will surrender sovereign power, he will master his passions, he will understand truth, and error will disappear in the world before the light of his knowledge, even as night flees before the spears of the sun. From the sea of evil, from the stinging spray of sickness, from the surge and swell of old age, from the angry waves of death, from these will he rescue the suffering world, and together they will sail away in the great ship of knowledge. He will know where it takes its rise, that swift, wonderful, beneficent river, the river of duty; he will reveal its course, and those who are tortured by thirst will come and drink of its waters. To those tormented by sorrow, to those enslaved by the senses, to those wandering in the forest of existence like travellers who have lost their way, he will point out the road to salvation. To those burning with the fire of passion, he will be the cloud that brings refreshing rain; armed with the true law, he will go to the prison of desires where all creatures languish, and he will break down the evil gates. For he who will have perfect understanding will set the world free.[7]

Asita's predictions unsettled Shuddodana. Wanting his son to follow in his footsteps and become a king, he decided never to let Siddhartha out of the palace, so that he would not witness the human suffering in the outside world. And so, from a very young age, Shuddodana always made sure that his son was given anything he wanted: a luxurious lifestyle, servants, and three palaces of his own. King Shuddodana even made sure to remove the sick, the aged, and the suffering from public view for fear that it would upset his son.

Yet as the prince grew, he became weary of his rich lifestyle. He found himself not very happy, and came to believe that perhaps material wealth is not the be-all and end-all in life. And when he met an old man during one of his trips outside the palace (despite all his father's efforts to hide them from him), Siddhartha was so depressed by the nature of human suffering that he decided to escape and go and live life as an ascetic. During his quest for enlightenment – the state free from ignorance, desire and suffering – he decided to pursue an extreme approach of total deprivation of worldly goods, including food. But after nearly starving himself to death, Siddhartha came to realise that this wasn't the way to achieve enlightenment. Instead, it was the state of mind that needed training.

And so, at the age of 35, Siddhartha sat down under a bodhi tree and began practising meditation, a training of the mind to achieve a calm awareness of one's body functions, feelings, and consciousness, and stopped treating his body cruelly in the process. And after only 49 days of meditation, Siddhartha achieved enlightenment and became known as the Buddha, or the 'Awakened One'.

By becoming enlightened, the Buddha is believed to have realised true insights into the nature and cause of human suffering – which was ignorance of the natural cycle of birth, ageing, illness and death – and the way to eliminate it. The realisation and the way to cessation of human suffering were later named 'The Four Noble Truths', which are:[8]

The Nature of Suffering. This represents the knowledge of suffering in the world, including birth, ageing, illness, and death. It also includes, but is not limited to, lamentation, pain, grief, despair, separation from what is pleasing, not getting what one wants, and clinging to what is not permanent.

The Suffering's Origin. This represents the knowledge of the origin of each of our sufferings, which includes craving for sensual pleasures, craving for existence, and craving extermination.

The Suffering's Cessation. This represents the knowledge of the end of suffering; it is the giving up and relinquishing of craving, as well as non-reliance on it.

The Path. This is the knowledge of the way leading to the cessation of suffering, including having right view, right intention, right speech, right action, right livelihood, right effort, right mindfulness, and right concentration.

Although the Buddha never denied that there's happiness in the world (he often spoke of the happiness that comes from friends and family), to him happiness was impermanent; and when one inevitably loses the things that make one happy, one suffers. In other words, according to the Buddha, the pursuit of happiness itself is suffering, but people are unaware of this because they are distracted by temporary pleasures. And since want is insatiable in itself (when you have something you want, you always want more), the true path towards supreme happiness – which is really the end of suffering – is to follow the *middle path*: the process of avoiding the extreme of indulging one's desires and the opposite extreme of torturing one's mind and body unnecessarily and unreasonably. The middle path involves, for example, engaging in regular meditation and the practising of loving kindness and compassion, which is the desire for the happiness and well-being of others. By following the middle path one can achieve a state of mindfulness whereby feelings such as desire, ill-will, or wants are realised to be nothing but thoughts. And once we can realise and be aware that they are just thoughts, we can let them go.[9]

'The Buddha said,' added my grandmother, 'do not dwell in the past; do not dream of the future; concentrate the mind on the present moment. The nature of the world is impermanent, and the more we cling on to anything that makes us happy, the unhappier we will be in the future. The mind is everything. What you think, you become.' My own personal Yoda ended the same way she started: with a Duchenne smile.

And so maybe it wasn't Philip Brickman and colleagues who first discovered that people adapt to changes in life events. It probably wasn't Richard Easterlin who was the first to conclude that economic growth for all increases the happiness of no one. And it definitely wasn't Daniel Kahneman and David Schkade who were the first to discover that attention is everything.

It was my 90-year-old grandmother. No, sorry. Scratch that. It was actually the Buddha who first discovered them over 2,500 years ago.

And the results generated by the happiness data are substantial proofs that he was right all along, that craving leads to suffering and, when our sufficient needs are met, happiness is nothing more than a state of mind, and one that we can train, given effort and time.

And that's perhaps the most radical truth of all.

NOTES

Chapter 1: The pursuit

1   This story was narrated to me in 2004 by John Bennett when we were attending a conference in Oxford together.

2   'Cognitive' refers to 'the process of thought', to logical reasoning.

3   Simon, H.A., 1982.

4   See Kahneman, D., Frederick, S., 2002.

5   See, for example, Damasio, H., Grabowski, T., Frank, R., Galaburda, A.M., Damasio, A.R., 1994. And also Loewenstein, G.F., Weber, E.U., Hsee, C.K., Welch, E.S., 2001. Although Gerd Gigerenzer would be one to argue that heuristic is not irrational (see Gigerenzer, G., Todd, P.M., and the ABC Research Group, 1999).

6   Gilbert, D.T., 2006a.

7   This is the idea of 'status quo bias' (people's tendency not to change behaviours unless the incentive to change is compelling). See, e.g., Samuelson, W., Zeckhauser, R.J., 1988.

8   Wilson, T.D., 2002.

9   Kahneman, D., Wakker, P.P., Sarin, R., 1997.

10 Redelmeier, D., Kahneman, D., 1996.

11 Ibid.

12 See also Lehrer, J., 2009.

13 Malcolm Gladwell argues in his 2008 book, *Outliers: The Story of Success*, that people will become experts in an area only when they have already spent at least 10,000 hours practising it.

14 Scott, J., 2000.

15 Brehm, J.W., 1966.

16 Ibid. See also Frey, D., 1981.

17 Gilbert, D.T., Pinel, E.C., Wilson, T.D., Blumberg, S.J., Wheatley, T.P., 1998.

18 Wilson, T.D., Wheatley, T.P., Meyers, J.M., Gilbert, D.T., Axsom, D., 2000.

Chapter 2: Happiness – what has science got to do with it?

1   Bob was a builder.

2   The amount is taken from the UK's Fatal Accidents Act, 1976. This £10,000 payment 'is designed to provide some compensation for the non-pecuniary losses associated with bereavement. It is only available to the husband or wife of the deceased, or, if the deceased was unmarried and a minor, to the parents. It does not give children a claim for the death of a parent.' Elliott, C., Quinn, F., 2005, p. 350.

3   The algorithm simply involves asking people to respond to questions about pleasure, such as: 'How strong is the pleasure?' and 'How long will a pleasure last?', for example. Bentham, J., 1789.

4   Robbins, L.C., 1938. And Hicks, J., 1934.

5   The terms 'happiness', 'life satisfaction', 'welfare' and 'mental well-being' have been used interchangeably by many researchers in the field.

6   While psychologists have given different definitions to different measures of happiness – e.g., life satisfaction is thought to be more of a measure of cognitive well-being (past, present and future), and happiness is more of a measure of affective well-being such as moods and emotions – all measures have been shown to be highly correlated with one another. This leads to the assumption that many of these happiness measures can therefore be used interchangeably in the analysis of human well-being.

7   Balatsky, G., Diener, E., 1993.

8   Sandvik, E., Diener, E., Seidlitz, L., 1993.

9   Goldings, H.J., 1954.

10   Eckman, P., Davidson, R.J., Friesen, W.V., 1990.

11   Shedler, J., Mayman, M., Manis, M., 1993.

12   Sales, S.M., House, J., 1971.

13   Davidson, R., 2000.

14   Davidson, R.J., Jackson, D.C., Kalin, N.H., 2000.

15   Danner, D.D., Snowdon, D.A., Frieson, W.V., 2001.

16   Taylor, D.H., Hassellblad, V., Henley, S.J., Thun, M.J., Sloan, F.A., 2002.

17   Friedman, M., 1957.

18   Duesenberry, J.S., 1949.

19   Frank, R.H., 2005.

20   Miller, R.L., 1994.

21   Ng, Y.-K., 1997.

22   McKelvey, R.D., Zavoina, W., 1975.

23 Sandvik, E., Diener, E., Seidlitz, L., 1993.

24 Van Praag, B.M.S., 1991.

25 Many economists working on happiness in the early 1990s, including Andrew Oswald, found it extremely tough to publish their work in economic journals. The tide turned, however, after 1997 when there was a big surge of research articles looking at various determinants of happiness.

26 Further refinements of McKelvey and Zavoina's ordered probit include, for example, McCullagh's ordered logit model (McCullagh, P., 1980), Boes and Winkelmann's generalised threshold ordered probit and ordered logit (Boes, S., Winkelmann, R., 2006), and Ferrer-i-Carbonell and Frijters' ordered logit with fixed effects (Ferrer-i-Carbonell, A., Frijters, P., 2004).

27 Over 460 journal articles on happiness were published between 1996 and 2008. Of those, over 170 were published between 2005 and 2008. For a comprehensive review of the literature, see Kahneman, D., Krueger, A.B., 2006.

Chapter 3: Money can't buy me love, but can it buy me happiness?

1 For a discussion on the philosophy of the pursuit of happiness and wealth around the world, see Oliver, J., 2007.

2 Easterlin, R.A., 1974.

3 The Gallup Poll.

4 Easterlin, R.A., 1995.

5 Easterlin, R.A., 2005.

6 Two of the leading authors recently rejecting the Easterlin Paradox are Justin Wolfers and Betty Stevenson (Wolfers, J., Stevenson, B., 2008).

7 For Richard Easterlin's own explanation of the contradictions made by the updated evidence, see his interview in VOX: http://www.voxeu.org/index.php?q=node/3439

8 After all, I'm only 5'3".

9 This example comes from Frank, R.H., 1999.

10 A similar idea is discussed in Powdthavee, N., 2007a.

11 Clark, A.E., Oswald, A.J., 1996.

12 Similar results are obtained using American (Hamermesh, D.S., 1977), Canadian (Lévy-Garboua, L., Montmarquette, C., 2004), and

British data sets (Sloane, P.J., Williams, H., 2000).

13 Ferrer-i-Carbonell, A., 2005.

14 Luttmer, E.F.P., 2005.

15 Knight, J., Song, L., Gunatilaka, R., 2009.

16 There are two separate studies conducted on the happiness of the South African people at the end of apartheid rule in 1994: Powdthavee, N., 2007a, and Kingdon, G., and Knight, J., 2007. For the Latin Americas and Russia, see Graham, C., and Pettinato, S., 2002.

17 Hirschman, A.O., 1973.

18 The theory on the impacts of income rank on well-being is first discussed in Parducci, A., 1965.

19 Brown, G.D.A., Gardner, J., Oswald, A.J., Qian, J., 2008.

20 A similar result is obtained using data of subjective economic status reported by villagers in Indonesia. See Powdthavee, N., 2009a. And also on life satisfaction, see Boyce et al., 2010.

21 Frank, R.H., 1985.

22 For a more comprehensive review of the literature, see Clark, A.E., Frijters, P., and Shields, M.A., 2008.

23 Especially Abraham Lincoln, who stood very tall at 6'4".

24 Buss, D.M., 1994.

25 Belot, M., Fidrmuc, J., 2009.

26 Case, A., Paxson, C., 2008.

27 Martel, L.F., Biller, H.B., 1987.

28 Case, A., Paxson, C., 2008.

29 Frank, R.H., 1985, p. 107.

30 Dawkins, R., 1976.

Chapter 4: The price of what money can't buy: Part I

1 http://www.slate.com/id/2137884

2 Oswald, A.J., 2006. Although, according to Andrew, his idea of a happiness equation was actually first popularised to the lay audience by the science editor of the BBC who, during one lunchtime news programme in 2000, decided to draw the equation out on the screen in the BBC studio and attempted to explain it in detail.

3 De Neve, K., Cooper, H., 1998.

4 Dolan, P., Peasgood, T., White, M., 2008.

5 Blanchflower, D.G., Oswald, A.J., 2008.

6   See, for example, Blanchflower, D.G., Oswald, A.J., 2004a; and
     Frey, B.S., Stutzer, A., 2005.

7   Clark, A.E., 1997.

8   Oswald, A.J., Powdthavee, N., 2007.

9   Stevenson, B., Wolfers, J., 2010.

10 This is only because education has the capacity to determine both
     an individual's health and income level – which can in turn affect
     how a person rates his or her subjective well-being.

11 Clark, A.E., Oswald, A.J., 1996.

12 Clark, A.E., 2003.

13 Stutzer, A., 2004.

14 Graham, C., Pettinato, S., 2002.

15 Blanchflower, D.G., Oswald, A.J., 2004a.

16 Smith, T.W., 2007.

17 Blanchflower, D.G., Oswald, A.J., 2004b.

18 Interested readers on the happiness correlates are encouraged to
     read Myers, D.G., 1993. See also Layard, R., 2005.

19 Burns, W.C., 1997.

20 Allen Paulos, J., 1996.

21 There is evidence that happier people earn more money in Russia.
     See Graham, C., Eggers, A., Sukhtankar, S., 2004.

22 For a more thorough discussion, see Powdthavee, N., 2010a.

23 There is a vast number of research articles in economics showing
     that schooling significantly increases our lifetime earnings. See, e.g.,
     Harmon, C., Walker, I., 1995.

24 See, e.g., Powdthavee, N., 2009b.

25 As in Oreopoulos, P., 2007.

26 Controlling for differences in age, year of the survey, and their birth
     year.

27 For readers who are interested in the technical side of econometrics,
     please refer to Wooldridge, J., 2002.

28 Oswald, A.J., Powdthavee, N., 2008a.

29 Oswald, A.J., Powdthavee, N., 2008b.

Chapter 5: The price of what money can't buy: Part II

1   Gardner, J., Oswald, A.J., 2007.

2   For more information on the measure on mental health (or the
     GHQ-12) used by Gardner and Oswald, see Goldberg, D.P., Geter,

R., Sartorius, N., Ustun, T.B., Piccinelli, M., Gureje, O., Rutter, C., 1997.

3 Oswald, A.J., Winkelmann, R., Powdthavee, N., 2010.

4 For a comprehensive review of psychological studies on deservingness, see Feather, N.T. 1999.

5 Frijters, P., Shields, M.A., Haisken-DeNew, J.P., 2004.

6 For example, as recently as December 1989, the East German mark was trading on the currency black market at 7M to 1DM (West German Deutschmark). Therefore, East German wages were increased to levels approaching 80 per cent of that of the West.

7 A natural occurrence of observable phenomena that closely replicates or duplicates the properties of a controlled experiment.

8 Diener, E., Emmons, R.A., Larsen, R.J., Griffin, S., 1985.

9 Darity, W., Goldsmith, A.H., 1996.

10 Powdthavee, N., 2010b.

11 The British Household Panel Survey (BHPS) is a nationally-representative sample of persons aged sixteen and over in 1991, who have been re-interviewed every year after. See also: http://www.iser.essex.ac.uk/survey/bhps for more details on the data set.

12 The process of using a variable that is unrelated to happiness but is related to income to predict income and then use that predicted income to predict happiness.

13 Or psychologists who work in the field of positive psychology, which is a branch in psychology that seeks to find ways to make normal life fulfilling.

14 Oswald, A.J., 1979.

15 Oswald. A.J., 1983.

16 Clark, A.E., Oswald, A.J., 1998.

17 See: http://www.guardian.co.uk/business/2004/may/08/4 for an interview with Andrew Oswald in the *Guardian*.

18 A similar version of this spoken quote of Andrew Oswald can be found in one of his published works: Oswald, A.J., 2003, p. 141.

19 Oswald, A.J., Powdthavee, N., 2008.

20 Dolan, P., Lee, H., King, D., Metcalfe, R., 2009.

21 Welsch, H., 2009.

22 Dolan, P., Peasgood, T., 2008.

23 Layard, R., 2005.

24 Putnam, R.D., 2001.

25 Helliwell, J.F., 2006.
26 Powdthavee, N., 2008.
27 Again, it should be noted that the terms 'happiness' and 'life satisfaction' are used interchangeably throughout this book.
28 Peasgood, T., 2007.
29 This is important, because people born with personality traits that make them daring and adventurous may also be happy but accident-prone.
30 Oswald, A.J., Powdthavee, N., 2010.
31 Powdthavee, N., Oswald, A.J., Wu, S., 2010.
32 Again, see Oswald, A.J., Powdthavee, N., 2008a.
33 Powdthavee, N., 2010b.
34 These reactions come mainly from comments given by *Daily Mail* readers when similar figures were published in July 2007.
35 Another more technical objection to the use of the shadow-pricing method to value non-market goods is that these monetary figures depend crucially on the assumption that the effect of income is linear across all income groups. This may not always be the case, e.g. at higher incomes you may need even more income to compensate for a negative shock in your life – given that you're already used to having such high income. Future research will need to come back to this in order to establish the true functional relationship between happiness and income.

Chapter 6: Does time really heal all wounds?

1   Brickman, P., Coates, D., Janoff-Bulman, R., 1978.
2   Brickman, P., Campbell, D.T., 1971.
3   Wortman, C., Coates, D., 1985.
4   Diener, E., Sandvik, E., Seidlitz, L., Diener, M., 1993.
5   Okun, M.A., George, L.K., 1984.
6   Diener, E., Wolsic, B., Fujita, F., 1995.
7   Lykken, D., Tellegen, A., 1996.
8   Feinman, S., 1978.
9   Riis, J., Lowenstein, G., Baron, J., Jepson, C., Fagerlin, A., Ubel, P.A., 2005.
10 There is work in economics on habit-formation, but that's not exactly the same as hedonic adaptation.
11 Biswas-Diener, R., Diener, E., 2005.

12 Clark, A.E., Georgellis, Y., Sanfey, P., 2001.

13 Lucas, R.E., Clark, A.E., Georgellis, Y., Diener, E., 2004.

14 For a classic study on the effect of unemployment on happiness, see Winkelmann, R., Winkelmann, L., 1998.

15 Clark, A.E., Diener, E., Georgellis, Y., Lucas, R.E., 2008.

16 A similar result is obtained when a measure of psychological distress is used instead of life satisfaction. See Gardner, J., Oswald, A.J., 2006.

17 Oswald, A.J., Powdthavee, N., 2008a.

18 Gardner, J., Oswald, A.J., 2006.

19 Powdthavee, N., 2009c. See also Angeles, L., 2009.

20 Frijters, P., Johnston, D.W., Shields, M.A., 2010.

21 Stutzer, A., Frey, B., 2008.

22 The only other winner of the Golden Slam is his wife, Steffi Graf.

23 A quote taken from Andre Agassi's autobiography *Open*, HarperCollins, 2009, p. 167.

24 Kahneman, D., Tversky, A., 1979.

25 Tversky, A., Kahneman, D., 1991.

26 Di Tella, R., Haisken-DeNew, J., MacCulloch, R., 2004.

27 However, it should be noted that Richard Easterlin and Anke Zimmerman found, using the same data set but a different estimation method, that there is indeed adaptation to marriage, but not a complete one (see Zimmerman, A., Easterlin, R.A., 2006).

28 For a comprehensive review of the literature on the impact of having children on happiness, see Powdthavee, N., 2009d.

29 Rayo, L., Becker, G.S., 2007.

30 Graham, L., Oswald, A.J., 2004.

31 Wilson, T.D., Gilbert, D.T., 2008. Avid readers should also read: Frederick, S., Loewenstein, G., 1999.

32 Another potential explanation as to why people may adapt faster to bereavement than to unemployment is that they can't blame themselves for their loved one's death and so they will adapt to it more easily. By contrast, they may find it harder to forgive themselves for being unable to find work.

33 Oswald, A.J., Powdthavee, N., 2008b.

34 For some examples of the positive experiences that could potentially last for a long time, see Csikszentmihalyi, M., 1991.

Chapter 7: Just as long as I'm not the only one

1   Levitt, S.D., Dubner, S.J., 2009.
2   All of these results can be found in Blanchflower, D.G., Oswald, A.J., 2004a; and Blanchflower, D.G., Oswald, A.J., 2004b.
3   http://www.truecrimexpo.co.za/
4   http://www.unodc.org/unodc/index.html?ref=menutop
5   Powdthavee, N., 2005.
6   Credit goes to Mat White for this.
7   Akerlof, G.A., 1970.
8   Akerlof, G.A., 1980.
9   Clark, A.E., 2003.
10 And ever since the publication of Clark's study in 2003, the same patterns of others' unemployment easing the mental pain of the unemployed have been replicated far and wide, including Germany (Clark, A.E., Knabe, A., Ratzel, S., 2009), South Africa (Powdthavee, N., 2007b), and Russia (Eggers, A., Gaddy, C., Graham, C., 2006).
11 Blanchflower, D.G., Oswald, A.J., Van Landegham, B., 2009.
12 Clark, A.E., Etilé, F., 2009.
13 For some evidence on the obesity spiral, see Christakis, N.A., Fowler, J.H., 2007.
14 Paluck, E.L., 2009.
15 After the genocide, the International Criminal Tribunal for Rwanda made a landmark conviction of the founders of RTLM radio station – known for its talk shows that made anti-Tutsi jokes and commentary – for the crime of genocide, arguing that it was the radio that instigated the hatred and 'set the stage' for genocide. See *Prosecutor vs. Nahimana, Barayagwiza, and Ngeze*, 2003, p. 29.
16 Goldstein, N.J., Cialdini, R.B., Griskevicius, V., 2008.
17 For an entire book on the idea of 'nudge' – or soft paternalism – see Thaler, R.H., Sunstein, C.R., 2008.

Chapter 8: Focusing illusions

1   You can read the comments from the *Daily Mail* website here: http://www.dailymail.co.uk/news/article-1163338/Children-dont-make-happy--says-expert-doesnt-any.html
2   And here for the online comments on the *New York Times* website: http://parenting.blogs.nytimes.com/2009/04/01/why-does-anyone-have-children/?hp

3   Much of the material of this chapter was first published in the
    Psychologist by the British Psychological Society; see Powdthavee, N.,
    2009d.

4   LeMasters, E.E., 1957.

5   For a classic review on the impact of children on marital
    satisfaction, see Glenn, N., McLanahan, S., 1982. See also Campbell,
    A., Converse, P.E., Rodgers, W.L., 1976.

6   For example, Kohler, H.-P., Behrman, J.R., Skytthe, A. 2005

7   See Powdthavee, N., 2009d.

8   Glenn, N.D., McLanahan, S., 1981.

9   Kahneman, D., Krueger, A.B., Schkade, D.A., Schwarz, N., Stone,
    A.A., 2004.

10 There is some evidence of a short-run increase in parents' happiness
    at the year of childbirth, but not thereafter (see Angeles, L., 2010).

11 Again, see the work by the psychonomists: Clark, A.E., Diener, E.,
    Georgellis, Y., Lucas, R.E., 2008.

12 Hitsch, G.J., Hortaçsu, A., Ariely, D., 2010. An earlier version
    (title: 'What makes you click? Mate preferences and matching
    outcome in online dating') containing a longer descriptive statistic
    of the data set, can be found on the Social Science Research
    Network (SSRN) website: http://papers.ssrn.com/sol3/Papers.
    cfm?abstract_id=895442

13 Readers interested in the better-than-average effect should also read
    Alicke, M.D., Govorun, O., 2005.

14 Gilbert, D.T., 2006a.

15 Crown, D.P., Marlowe, D., 1960. Social desirability bias is also
    the very reason why most happiness survey questions are
    self-completed.

16 You can read Dan's article in *Time* in 2006 (title: 'Does fatherhood
    make you happy?') online here: http://www.time.com/time/
    magazine/article/0,9171,1202940,00.html

17 Haidt, J., 2005.

18 Haidt, J., 2001, p. 2.

19 Schkade, D.A., Kahneman, D., 1998.

20 Kahneman, D., Kruger, A.B., Schkade, D.A., Schwarz, N., Stone,
    A.A., 2006.

21 Gilbert, D., 2006b.

22 White, M.P., Dolan, P., 2009.

Chapter 9: Why should we be happy?

1 Belliotti, R.A., 2003.

2 Rubin, G., 2009, *The Happiness Project: Or, Why I Spent a Year Trying to Sing in the Morning, Clean My Closets, Fight Right, Read Aristotle, and Generally Have More Fun*, Harper (US), Bantam; Hanson, R., 2009, *Buddha's Brain: The Practical Neuroscience of Happiness, Love, and Wisdom*, New Harbinger; Thaler, R.H., Sunstein, C.R., *Nudge: Improving Decisions about Health, Wealth and Happiness*, Penguin, UK; Leonsis, T., Danziger, L., Birndorf, C., 2010, *The Nine Rooms of Happiness: Loving Yourself, Finding Your Purpose, and Getting Over Life's Little Imperfections*, Voice; Gilbert, D.T., 2007, *Stumbling on Happiness*, Vintage.

3 Holstijn, A.J.W., 1957, p. 1.

4 Ludwig, A.M., 1992.

5 Martin, L.L., Ward, D.W., Achee, J.W., Wyer, R.S., 1993.

6 Isen, A.M., 1999.

7 See Isen, A.M., Daubman, K.A., Nowicki, G.P., 1987; Carnevale, P.J., Isen, A.M., 1986.

8 Amabile, T.M., Barsade, S.G., Mueller, J.S., Staw, B.M., 2005.

9 Sanna, L.J., Turley, K.J., Mark, M.M., 1996.

10 A similar finding of a positive effect of happiness on productivity has recently been replicated in a setting where performance-related pay is involved (see Oswald, A.J., Proto, E., Sgroi, D., 2009).

11 Lyubomirsky, S., Diener, E., King, L., 2005.

12 Thoresen, C.J., Kaplan, S.A., Barsky, A.P., Warren, C.R., de Chermont, K., 2003.

13 Diener, E., Nickerson, C., Lucas, R.E., Sandvik, E., 2002.

14 Marks, G.N., Fleming, N., 1999.

15 Harker, L.A., Keltner, D., 2001.

16 Staw, B.M., Sutton, R.I., Pelled, L.H., 1994.

17 Keltner, D., Kring, A., 1998.

18 Staw, B.M., Sutton, R.I., Pelled, L.H., 1994.

19 Thoits, P.A., Hewitt, L.N., 2001.

20 Ostir, G.V., Markides, K.S., Black, S.A., Goodwin, J.S., 2001.

21 Lyons, A., Chamberlain, K., 1994; Gil, K.M., Carson, J.W., Porter, L.S., Scipio, C., Bediako, S.M., Orringer, E., 2004.

22 Kirkcaldy, B., Furnham, A., 2000.

23 Devins, G.M., Mann, J., Mandin, H.P., Leonard, C., 1990; Levy, S.M.,

Lee, J., Bagley, C., Lippman, M., 1988.; Krause, J.S., Sternberg, M., Lottes, S., Maides, J., 1997.

24 Cunningham, M.R., 1988.

25 Hirt, E.R., Melton, R.J., McDonald, H.E., Harackiewicz, J.M., 1996.

26 Baron, R.A., 1993.

27 McClelland, D.C., Cheriff, A.D., 1997.

28 Blass, T., 2004.

29 Milgram, S., 1974.

30 Milgram, S., 1967.

31 Although Stanley Milgram never used this term himself.

32 Goyal, S., van der Leij, M., Moraga-González, J.S., 2006.

33 Fowler, J.H., Christakis, N.A., 2008.

34 Fowler, J.H., Christakis, N.A., 2009.

35 Powdthavee, N., 2009e.

36 Bolger, N., DeLongis, A., Kessler, R.C., Wethington, E., 1989.

37 Bolger, N., DeLongis, A., Kessler, R.C., Schilling, E.A., 1989.

38 Powdthavee, N., Vignoles, A., 2008.

39 Melton, R.J., 1995.

Chapter 10: Who gets to decide?

1 For an illustration of Bhutan's amazing achievement in social infrastructure, there were four hospitals in the whole of Bhutan in the 1950s, compared to 26 hospitals, 145 Basic Health Units and a network of some 450 outreach clinics in the 1990s.

2 Priesner, S., 2004.

3 McDonald, R., 2005.

4 See a discussion of Bhutan's public policies on the BBC's 'Bhutan's Happiness Formula': http://news.bbc.co.uk/1/hi/in_pictures/4782636.stm

5 Layard, R., 2006.

6 Stutzer, A., Frey, B., 2008.

7 Steele, G.R., 2006.

8 Veenhoven, R., 2000.

9 Thaler, R.H., Sunstein, C.R., 2008.

10 Sunstein, C., 2003. See also: Thaler, R.H., Sunstein, C.R., 2003.

11 Tversky, A., Kahneman, D., 1981. See also: Tversky, A., Kahneman, D., 1986.

12 Quattrone, G., Tversky, A., 1988.

13 Meyerowitz, B.E., Chaiken, S., 1987.

14 Drouvelis, M., Metcalfe, R., Powdthavee, N., 2010.

15 Bargh, J.A., Chen, M., Burrows, L., 1996.

16 Samuelson, W., Zeckhauser, R.J., 1988.

17 Selvin, S., 1975.

18 An easier way to look at the Monty Hall problem is to imagine three possible outcomes from our decision. Let's say we choose door A. If the car is behind door A, then the decision to switch door will be wrong. However, if the car is in fact behind door B or C, and Monty can open only a door that has a goat behind it, we have a 2/3 chance of winning a car if we switch. Thanks go to Somkiat Tangkitvanich and Samphan Rattana-Amornchai for showing me an easier way to explain this problem.

19 Thaler, R.H., 1980.

20 Festinger, L., 1957.

21 Kahneman, D., Knetsch, J., Thaler, R.H., 1991.

22 Samuelson, W., Zeckhauser, R.J., 1988.

23 Thaler, R.H., Benartzi, S., 2004.

24 Johnson, E.J., Goldstein, D.G., 2003.

25 Readers interested in libertarian paternalism are encouraged to read *Nudge* by Richard H. Thaler and Cass R. Sunstein, and *Predictably Irrational* by Dan Ariely (Ariely, D., 2008).

26 White, M.P., Dolan, P., 2009.

27 Frey, B.S., Stutzer, A., 2009.

28 For a recent debate on this topic, see Bok, D., 2010.

29 www.stiglitz-sen-fitoussi.fr/

30 http://blog.ted.com/2010/02/mindshift_round.php

Chapter 11: And the funny thing is?

1 For studies that use the happiness approach to value noise pollution and clean air, see Van Praag, B.M.S., Baarsma, B.E., 2005, and also Luechinger, S., 2009.

2 This project has already started. Robert Metcalfe, Paul Dolan and I have found that the September 11th attacks adversely affected the mental well-being of people who were interviewed post-9/11 in the UK. See Metcalfe, R., Powdthavee, N., Dolan, P., 2009.

3 Oswald, A.J., Wu, S., 2010.

4   The authors note that it's unusual that Louisiana, a state affected
     by Hurricane Katrina in 2005, ranks very highly in the happiness
     table. However, they argue that Louisiana showed up strongly before
     Katrina in a mental-health ranking done by Mental Health America
     and the Office of Applied Studies of the US Substance Abuse and
     Mental Health Service Administration.
5   Blanchflower, D.G., Oswald, A.J., 2008.
6   Steptoe, A., Wardle, J., 2005.
7   Harold, A.F., 1922, translated from the French by P.C. Blum, 1927
     (reprinted 2007).
8   *Dhammacakkappavattana Sutta*, 2000.
9   There's even scientific evidence to support the notion that
     meditation can help increase happiness. See Lutz, A., Brefczynski-
     Lewis, J., Johnstone, T., Davidson, R.J., 2008.

BIBLIOGRAPHY

Akerlof, G.A, 1970, 'The market for "lemons": quality uncertainty
and the market mechanism', *Quarterly Journal of Economics*, 84,
488–500

Agassi, A., 2009, *Open*, HarperCollins, p. 167

Akerlof, G.A., 1980, 'A theory of social customs, of which
unemployment may be one consequence', *Quarterly Journal of
Economics*, 94, 749–75

Alicke, M.D., Govorun, O., 2005, 'The better-than-average effect', in
M.D. Alicke, D.A. Dunning, J.I. Krueger (eds), *The Self in Social
Judgment*, CRC Press, pp. 85–106

Allen Paulos, J., 1996, *A Mathematician Reads the Newspaper*,
Penguin Books, p. 137

Amabile, T.M., Barsade, S.G., Mueller, J.S., Staw, B.M., 2005, 'Affect
and creativity at work', *Administrative Science Quarterly*, 50,
367–403

Angeles, L., 2009, 'Adaptation and anticipation effects to life events in
the United Kingdom', University of Glasgow, manuscript

Ariely, D., 2008, *Predictably Irrational: The Hidden Forces That Shape
Our Decisions*, HarperCollins

Balatsky, G., Diener, E., 1993, 'Subjective well-being among Russian
students', *Social Indicator Research*, 28, 225–43

Bargh, J.A., Chen, M., Burrows, L., 1996, 'Automaticity of social
behavior: direct effects of trait construct and stereotype activation
on action', *Journal of Personality and Social Psychology*, 71, 230–44

Baron, R.A., 1993, 'Interviewers' moods and evaluations of job
applications: the role of applicant qualifications', *Journal of
Applied Social Psychology*, 23, 253–71

Belliotti, R.A., 2003, *Happiness is Overrated*, Rowman & Littlefield
Publishers, Inc.

Belot, M., Fidrmuc, J., 2009, 'Anthropology of love: height and gender asymmetries in interethnic marriage', Oxford University, working paper

Bentham, J., 1789, *An Introduction to the Principles of Morals and Legislation*, London, Chapter 4

Biswas-Diener, R., Diener, E., 2005, 'Most people are pretty happy, but there is cultural variation: the Inughuit, the Amish, and the Maasai', *Journal of Happiness Studies*, 6, 205–26

Blanchflower, D.G., Oswald, A.J., 2004a, 'Well-being over time in Britain and the USA', *Journal of Public Economics*, 88, 1359–86

Blanchflower, D.G., Oswald, A.J., 2004b, 'Money, sex, and happiness: an empirical evidence', *Scandinavian Journal of Economics*, 106, 393–416

Blanchflower, D.G., Oswald, A.J., 2008, 'Is well-being U-shaped over the life cycle?' *Social Science and Medicine*, 66, 1733–49

Blanchflower, D.G., Oswald, A.J., 2008, 'Hypertension and happiness across nations', *Journal of Health Economics*, 27, 218–33

Blanchflower, D.G., Oswald, A.J., Van Landegham, B., 2009, 'Imitative obesity and relative utility', *Journal of European Economic Association*, 7, 528–38

Blass, T., 2004, *The Man Who Shocked The World: The Life and Legacy of Stanley Milgram*, Perseus Books

Boes, S., Winkelmann, R., 2006, 'Ordered response models', *Advances in Statistical Analysis*, 90, 165–79

Bok, D.C., 2010, *The Politics of Happiness: What Government Can Learn from the New Research on Well-Being*, Princeton University Press, Princeton NJ

Bolger, N., DeLongis, A., Kessler, R.C., Schilling, E.A., 1989, 'Effects of daily stress on negative moods', *Journal of Personality and Social Psychology*, 57, 808–18

Bolger, N., DeLongis, A., Kessler, R.C., Wethington, E., 1989, 'The contagion of stress across multiple roles', *Journal of Marriage and the Family*, 51, 175–83

Boyce, C.J., Brown, G.D.A., Moore, S.C., 2010, 'Money and happiness: rank of income, not income, affects life satisfaction', *Psychological Science*, 21, 471–75

Brehm, J.W., 1966, A *Theory of Psychological Reactance*, Academic Press, New York

Brickman, P., Campbell, D.T., 1971, 'Hedonic relativism and planning the good society', in M.H. Appley (ed.), *Adaptation-level theory*, New York, Academic Press, pp. 287–305

Brickman, P., Coates, D., Janoff-Bulman, R., 1978, 'Lottery winners and accident victims: Is happiness relative?', *Journal of Personality and Social Psychology*, 36, 917–27

Brown, G.D.A., Gardner, J., Oswald, A.J., Qian, J., 2008, 'Does wage rank affect employees' well-being?', *Industrial Relations*, 47(3), 355–89

Burns, W.C., 1997, *Spurious Correlations*, retrieved February 2010, from: http://www.burns.com/wcbspurcorl.htm

Buss, D.M., 1994, *The Evolution of Desire: Strategies of Human Mating*, Basic Books

Campbell, A., Converse, P.E., Rodgers, W.L., 1976, *The Quality of American Life*, Russell Sage Foundation, New York

Carnevale, P.J., Isen, A.M., 1986, 'The influence of positive affect and visual access on the discovery of integrative solutions in bilateral negotiation', *Organizational Behavior and Human Decision Processes*, 37, 1–13

Case, A., Paxson, C., 2008, 'Stature and status: height, ability, and labor market outcomes', *Journal of Political Economy*, 116, 499–532

Christakis, N.A., Fowler, J.H., 2007, 'The spread of obesity in a large social network over 32 years', *The New England Journal of Medicine*, 357, 370–79

Clark, A.E., 1997, 'Job satisfaction and gender: why are women so happy at work?', *Labour Economics*, 4, 341–72

Clark, A.E., 2003, 'Unemployment as a social norm: psychological evidence from panel data', *Journal of Labor Economics*, 21, 323–51

Clark, A.E., Etilé, F., 2009, 'Happy house: spousal weight and individual well-being', Paris School of Economics, manuscript

Clark, A.E., Oswald, A.J., 1996, 'Satisfaction and comparison income', *Journal of Public Economics*, 61, 359–81

Clark, A.E., Oswald, A.J., 1998, 'Comparison-concave utility and following behavior and social science setting', *Journal of Public Economics*, 70, 133–55

Clark, A.E., Diener, E., Georgellis, Y., Lucas, R.E., 2008, 'Lags and leads in life satisfaction: a test of the baseline hypothesis', *Economic Journal*, 118, F222–43

Clark, A.E., Frijters, P., and Shields, M.A., 2008, 'Relative income, happiness and utility: An explanation for the Easterlin Paradox and other puzzles', *Journal of Economic Literature*, 46(1), 95–144

Clark, A.E., Georgellis, Y., Sanfey, P., 2001, 'Scarring: the psychological impact of past unemployment', *Economica*, 68, 221–41

Clark, A.E., Knabe, A., Ratzel, S., 2009, 'Unemployment as a social norm in Germany', *Journal of Applied Social Science Studies*, 129, 251–60

Crown, D.P., Marlowe, D., 1960, 'A new scale of social desirability independent of psychopathology', *Journal of Consulting Psychology*, 24, 349–54

Csikszentmihalyi, M., 1991, *Flow: The Psychology of Optimal Experience*, Harper Perennial

Cunningham, M.R., 1988, 'Does happiness mean friendliness? Induced mood and heterosexual self-disclosure', *Personality and Social Psychology Bulletin*, 14, 283–97

Damasio, H., Grabowski, T., Frank, R., Galaburda, A.M., Damasio, A.R., 1994, 'The return of Phineas Gage: Clues about the brain from the skull of a famous patient', *Science*, 263, 1102–05

Danner, D.D., Snowdon, D.A., Frieson, W.V., 2001, 'Positive emotions in early life and longevity: findings from the nun study', *Journal of Personality and Social Psychology*, 80(5), 804–13

Darity, W., Goldsmith, A.H., 1996, 'Social psychology, unemployment and macroeconomics', *Journal of Economic Perspectives*, 10, 121–40

Davidson, R., 2000, 'Affective style, psychopathology and resilience: brain mechanisms and plasticity', *American Psychologist*, 55, 1196–1214

Davidson, R.J., Jackson, D.C., Kalin, N.H., 2000, 'Emotion, plasticity, context and regulation: Perspectives from affective neuroscience', *Psychological Bulletin*, 126, 890–906

Dawkins, R., 1976, *The Selfish Gene*, Oxford University Press

De Neve, K., Cooper, H., 1998, 'The happy personality: a meta analysis of 137 personality traits and subjective well-being', *Psychological Bulletin*, 125, 197–229

Devins, G.M., Mann, J., Mandin, H.P., Leonard, C., 1990, 'Psychosocial predictors of survival in end-stage renal disease', *Journal of Nervous and Mental Disease*, 178, 127–33

Dhammacakkappavattana Sutta, or the Buddha's discourse (trans. Bodhi), 2000, pp. 1843–7

Di Tella, R., Haisken-DeNew, J., MacCulloch, R., 2004, 'Happiness adaptation to income and to status in an individual panel', available at SSRN: http://ssrn.com/abstract=760368

Diener, E., Emmons, R.A., Larsen, R.J., Griffin, S., 1985, 'The satisfaction with life scale', *Journal of Personality Assessment*, 49, 71–5

Diener, E., Nickerson, C., Lucas, R.E., Sandvik, E., 2002, 'Dispositional affect and job outcomes', *Social Indicators Research*, 59, 229–59

Diener, E., Sandvik, E., Seidlitz, L., Diener, M., 1993, 'The relationship between income and subjective well-being: Relative or absolute?', *Social Indicators Research*, 28, 195–223

Diener, E., Wolsic, B., Fujita, F., 1995, 'Physical attractiveness and subjective well-being', *Journal of Personality and Social Psychology*, 69, 120–29

Dolan, P., Peasgood, T., 2008, 'Measuring well-being for public policy: preferences or experiences', *Journal of Legal Studies*, S37, S5–31

Dolan, P., Peasgood, T., White, M., 2008, 'Do we really know what makes us happy? A review of the economic literature on the factors associated with subjective well-being', *Journal of Economic Psychology*, 29, 94–122

Dolan, P., Lee, H., King, D., Metcalfe, R., 2009, 'Valuing health directly', *British Medical Journal*, 339, 371–3

Drouvelis, M., Metcalfe, R., Powdthavee, N., 2010, 'Priming cooperation in social dilemma games', Department of Economics and Related Studies, University of York, manuscript

Duesenberry, J.S., 1949, *Income, saving and the theory of consumer behavior*, Harvard University Press, Cambridge MA

Easterlin, R.A., 1974, 'Does economic growth improve the human lot?', in P.A. David, M.W. Reder (eds), *Nations and Households in Economic Growth: Essays in Honor of Moses Abramovitz*, Academic Press Inc., New York

Easterlin, R.A., 1995, 'Will raising the incomes of all increase the happiness of all?', *Journal of Economic Behavior and Organization*, 27, 35–47

Easterlin, R.A., 2005, 'Feeding the illusion of growth and happiness: A reply to Hagerty and Veenhoven', *Social Indicators Research*, 74, 429–43

Eckman, P., Davidson, R.J., Friesen, W.V., 1990, 'The Duchenne smile: Emotional expression and brain physiology II', *Journal of Personality and Social Psychology*, 58(2), 342–53

Eggers, A., Gaddy, C., Graham, C., 2006, 'Well-being and unemployment in Russia in the 1990s: Can society's suffering be individual's solace?', *Journal of Socio-Economics*, 35, 209–42

Elliott, C., Quinn, F., 2005, *Tort Law*, Longman, London, p. 350

Feather, N.T., 1999, *Values, Achievement, and Justice: Studies in the Psychology of Deservingness (Critical Issues in Social Justice)*, Springer

Feinman, S., 1978, 'The blind as "ordinary people"', *Journal of Visual Impairment and Blindness*, 72, 231–8

Ferrer-i-Carbonell, A., Frijters, P., 2004, 'How important is methodology for the estimates of the determinants on happiness?', *Economic Journal*, 114, 641–59

Ferrer-i-Carbonell, A., 2005, 'Income and well-being: an empirical analysis of the comparison income effect', *Journal of Public Economics*, 89, 997–1019

Festinger, L., 1957, *A Theory of Cognitive Dissonance*, Stanford University Press, Stanford CA

Fowler, J.H., Christakis, N.A., 2008, 'Dynamic spread of happiness in a large social network: longitudinal analysis over 20 years in the Framingham Heart Study', *British Medical Journal*, 337:a, 2338

Fowler, J.H., Christakis, N.A., 2009, *Connected: The Surprising Power of Our Social Networks and How They Shape Our Lives*, Little, Brown & Co.

Frank, R.H., 1985, 'The demand for unobservable and nonpositional goods', *American Economic Review*, 75(1), 101–16

Frank, R.H., 1999, *Luxury Fever: Money and Happiness in an Era of Excess*, Princeton University Press, Princeton NJ

Frank, R.H., 2005, 'The mysterious disappearance of James Duesenberry', *New York Times*, *Economic Scene* (June issue)

Frederick, S., Loewenstein, G., 1999, 'Hedonic adaptation', in E. Diener, N. Schwartz, D. Kahneman (eds), *Hedonic psychology: Scientific approaches to enjoyment, suffering, and well-being*, Russell Sage Foundation Press, New York, pp. 302–29

Frey, D., 1981, 'Reversible and irreversible decisions: Preference for constant information as a function of attractiveness of decision alternatives', *Personality and Social Psychology Bulletin*, 7, 621–6

Frey, B.S., Stutzer, A., 2005, 'Testing theories of happiness', in L. Bruni, L. Porta (eds), *Economics and Happiness: Framing the Analysis*, Oxford University Press, pp. 116–45

Frey, B.S., Stutzer, A., 2009, 'Should national happiness be maximised?', in A. Krishna Dutt (ed.), *Happiness, Economics and Politics: New Lessons for Old Problems*, Edward Elgar Publishing, pp. 301–23

Friedman, M., 1957, *A theory of consumption function*, Princeton University Press, Princeton NJ

Frijters, P., Shields, M.A., Haisken-Denew, J.P., 2004, 'Money does matter! Evidence from increasing real incomes in East Germany following reunification', *American Economic Review*, 94, 730–41

Frijters, P., Johnston, D.W., Shields, M.A., 2010, 'Happiness dynamics with quarterly life event data', *Scandinavian Journal of Economics*, forthcoming

Gardner, J., Oswald, A.J., 2006, 'Do divorcing couples become happier by breaking up?', *Journal of Royal Statistical Society: Series A*, 169, 319–36

Gardner, J., Oswald, A.J., 2007, 'Money and mental well-being: a longitudinal study of medium-sized lottery wins', *Journal of Health Economics*, 26, 49–60

Gigerenzer, G., Todd, P.M., and the ABC Research Group, 1999, *Simple Heuristics That Make Us Smart*, Oxford University Press

Gilbert, D.T., 2006a, *Stumbling on Happiness*, HarperCollins

Gilbert, D.T., 2006b, 'Does fatherhood make you happy?', article in *The Times*

Gilbert, D.T., Pinel, E.C., Wilson, T.D., Blumberg, S.J., Wheatley, T.P., 1998, 'Immune neglect: A source of durability bias in affective forecasting', *Journal of Personality and Social Psychology*, 75, 617–38

Gil, K.M., Carson, J.W., Porter, L.S., Scipio, C., Bediako, S.M., Orringer, E., 2004, 'Daily mood and stress predict pain, health care use, and work activity in African American adults with sickle-cell disease', *Health Psychology*, 23, 267–74

Gladwell, M., 2005, *Blink*, Penguin

Gladwell, M., 2008, *Outliers: The Story of Success*, Allen Lane

Glenn, N.D., McLanahan, S., 1981, 'The effect of children on the psychological well-being of older adults', *Journal of Marriage and Family*, 43, 409–21

Glenn, N.D., McLanahan, S., 1982, 'Children and marital happiness: a further specification of the relationship', *Journal of Marriage and the Family*, 44, 63–72

Goldberg, D.P., Geter, R., Sartorius, N., Ustun, T.B., Piccinelli, M., Gureje, O., Rutter, C., 1997, 'The validity of two versions of the GHQ in the WHO study of mental illness in general health care', *Psychological Medicine*, 27:1, 191–7

Goldings, H.J., 1954, 'On the avowal and projection of happiness', *Journal of Personality*, 23, 30–47

Goldstein, N.J., Cialdini, R.B., Griskevicius, V., 2008, 'A room with a viewpoint: using social norms to motivate environmental conservation in hotels', *Journal of Consumer Research*, 35, 472–82

Goyal, S., van der Leij, M., Moraga-González, J.S., 2006, 'Economics: an emerging small world', *Journal of Political Economy*, 114, 403–12

Graham, C., Pettinato, S., 2002, *Happiness and Hardship: Opportunity and Security in New Market Economies*, Brooking Institution Press, Washington DC

Graham, C., Eggers, A., Sukhtankar, S., 2004, 'Does happiness pay? An exploration based on panel data from Russia', *Journal of Economic Behavior and Organization*, 55, 319–42

Graham, L., Oswald, A.J., 2004, 'Hedonic capital', Department of Economics, University College London, manuscript

Haidt, J. 2001, 'The emotional dog and its rational tail: a social intuitionist approach to moral judgement', *Psychological Review*, 108, 814–34

Haidt, J. 2005, *The Happiness Hypothesis: Putting Ancient Wisdom to the Test of Modern Science*, Arrow Books Ltd

Hamermesh, D.S., 1977, 'Economic Aspects of Job Satisfaction', in O. Ashenfelter, W. Oates (eds), *Essays in Labor Market Analysis*, John Wiley, New York

Harker, L.A., Keltner, D., 2001, 'Expressions of positive emotion in women's college year book pictures and their relationship to personality and life outcomes across adulthood', *Journal of Personality and Social Psychology*, 80, 112–24

Harmon, C., Walker, I., 1995, 'Estimates of the return to schooling for the United Kingdom', *American Economic Review*, 85, 1278–86

Harold, A.F., 1922, translated from the French by P.C. Blum, 1927 (reprinted 2007), *The Life of Buddha*, BiblioBazaar, p. 18

Helliwell, J.F., 2006, 'Well-being, social capital and public policy: What's new?', *Economic Journal*, 116, C34–45

Hicks, J., 1934, 'A Reconsideration of the Theory of Value, I', *Economica*, 1, 52–75

Hirschman, A.O., 1973, 'Changing tolerance for income inequality in the course of economic development', *Quarterly Journal of Economics*, 87(4), 544–66

Hirt, E.R., Melton, R.J., McDonald, H.E., Harackiewicz, J.M., 1996, 'Processing goals, task interest, and the mood-performance relationship: a meta-analysis', *Journal of Personality and Social Psychology*, 71, 245–61

Hitsch, G.J., Hortaçsu, A., Ariely, D., 2010, 'Matching and sorting in online dating', *American Economic Review*, forthcoming

Holstijn, A.J.W., 1957, 'The psychological development of Vincent Van Gogh', *Journal of Mental Science*, 103, 107

Isen, A.M., Daubman, K.A., Nowicki, G.P., 1987, 'Positive affect facilitates creative problem solving', *Journal of Personality and Social Psychology*, 52, 1121–31

Isen, A.M., 1999, 'On the relationship between affect and creative problem solving', in S.W. Russ (ed.), *Affect, Creative Experience and Psychological Adjustment*, Brunner/Mazel, Philadelphia, pp. 3–18

Johnson, E.J., Goldstein, D.G., 2003, 'Do defaults save lives?', *Science*, 302, 1338–9

Kahneman, D., Frederick, S., 2002, 'Representativeness revisited: attribute substitution in intuitive judgment', in T. Gilovich, D. Griffin, D. Kahneman (eds), *Heuristics of Intuitive Judgment: Extensions and Applications*, Cambridge University Press, New York

Kahneman, D., Knetsch, J., Thaler, R.H., 1991, 'Anomalies: the endowment effect, loss aversion, and status quo bias', *Journal of Economic Perspectives*, 5, 193–206

Kahneman, D., Krueger, A.B., 2006, 'Developments in the measurement of subjective well-being', *Journal of Economic Perspectives*, 5, 193–206

Kahneman, D., Krueger, A.B., Schkade, D.A., Schwarz, N., Stone, A.A., 2004, 'A survey method for characterizing daily life experience: The day reconstruction method', *Science*, 306, 1776–80

Kahneman, D., Kruger, A.B., Schkade, D.A., Schwarz, N., Stone, A.A., 2006, 'Would you be happier if you were richer?', *Science*, 312, 1908–10

Kahneman, D., Tversky, A., 1979, 'Prospect theory: an analysis of decision under risk', *Econometrica*, 47, 263–91

Kahneman, D., Wakker, P.P., Sarin, R., 1997, 'Back to Bentham? Explorations of experienced utility', *Quarterly Journal of Economics*, 112(2), 375–405

Keltner, D., Kring, A., 1998, 'Emotion, social function, and psychopathology', *Review of General Psychology*, 2, 320–42

Kingdon, G., Knight, J., 2007, 'Community, comparisons and subjective well-being in a divided society', *Journal of Economic Behavior and Organization*, 64, 69–90

Kirkcaldy, B., Furnham, A., 2000, 'Positive affectivity, psychological well-being, accident- and traffic-deaths and suicide: an international comparison', *Studia Psychologica*, 42, 97–104

Knight, J., Song, L., Gunatilaka, R., 2009, 'Subjective well-being and its determinants in rural China', *China Economic Review*, 20, 635–49

Kohler, H-P., Behrman, J.R., Skytthe, A., 2005, 'Partner + children = happiness: the effects of partnerships and fertility on well-being', *Population and Development Review*, 31, 407–55

Krause, J.S., Sternberg, M., Lottes, S., Maides, J., 1997, 'Mortality after spinal-cord injury: an 11-year prospective study', *Archives of Physical Medicine and Rehabilitation*, 78, 815–21

Layard, R., 2005, *Happiness: Lessons from a New Science*, Penguin, London

Layard, R., 2006, 'Happiness and public policy: a challenge to the profession', *Economic Journal*, 116, C24–33

Lehrer, J., 2009, *The Decisive Moment: How the Brain Makes Up Its Mind*, Canongate, Edinburgh

LeMasters, E.E., 1957, 'Parenthood as crisis', *Marriage and Family Living*, 19, 352–5

Levitt, S.D., Dubner, S.J., 2009, *Superfreakonomics: global cooling, patriotic prostitutes, and why suicide bombers should buy life insurance*, Allen Lane, p. 14

Levy, S.M., Lee, J., Bagley, C., Lippman, M., 1988, 'Survival hazard analysis in first recurrent breast cancer patients: seven-year follow up', *Psychosomatic Medicine*, 50, 520–28

Lévy-Garboua, L., Montmarquette, C., 2004, 'Reported job satisfaction: What does it mean?', *Journal of Socio-Economics*, 33, 135–51

Loewenstein, G.F., Weber, E.U., Hsee, C.K., and Welch, E.S., 2001, 'Risk as feelings', *Psychological Bulletin*, 127, 267

Lucas, R.E., Clark, A.E., Georgellis, Y., Diener, E., 2004, 'Unemployment alters the set point for life satisfaction', *Psychological Science*, 15, 8–14

Ludwig, A.M., 1992, 'Creative achievement and psychopathology: comparisons among professions', *American Journal of Psychotherapy*, 46, 330–56

Luechinger, S., 2009, 'Valuing air quality using the life satisfaction approach', *Economic Journal*, 119, 482–515

Luttmer, E.F.P., 2005, 'Neighbours as negatives: relative earnings and well-being', *Quarterly Journal of Economics*, 120, 963–1002

Lutz, A., Brefczynski-Lewis, J., Johnstone, T., Davidson, R.J., 2008, 'Regulation of the Neural Circuitry of Emotion by Compassion Meditation: Effects of Meditative Expertise', *PloS ONE*, 3, e1897

Lykken, D., Tellegen, A., 1996, 'Happiness is a stochastic phenomenon', *Psychological Science*, 7, 186–9

Lyons, A., Chamberlain, K., 1994, 'The effects of minor events, optimism and self-esteem on health', *British Journal of Clinical Psychology*, 33, 559–70

Lyubomirsky, S., Diener, E., King, L., 2005, 'The benefits of frequent positive affect: does happiness lead to success?', *Psychological Bulletin*, 131, 803–55

Marks, G.N., Fleming, N., 1999, 'Influences and consequences of well-being among Australian young people: 1980–1995', *Social Indicators Research*, 46, 301–23

Martel, L.F., Biller, H.B., 1987, *Stature and Stigma: The Biopsychosocial Development of Short Males*, Lexington Books, Lexington MA

Martin, L.L., Ward, D.W., Achee, J.W., Wyer, R.S., 1993, 'Mood as input: people have to interpret the motivational implications of their moods', *Journal of Personality and Social Psychology*, 64, 317–26

McClelland, D.C., Cheriff, A.D., 1997, 'The immunoenhancing effects of humor on secretory IgA and resistance to respiratory infection', *Psychology and Health*, 12, 329–44

McCullagh, P., 1980, 'Regression models for ordinal data', *Journal of the Royal Statistical Society Series B*, 42, 109–42

McDonald, R., 2005, 'Towards a new conceptualization of Gross National Happiness and its foundations', *Journal of Bhutan Studies*, 12, 23–46

McKelvey, R.D., Zavoina, W., 1975, 'A statistical model for the analysis of ordinal level dependent variables', *Journal of Mathematical Sociology*, 4, 103–20

Melton, R.J., 1995, 'The role of positive affect in syllogism performance', *Personality and Social Psychology Bulletin*, 21, 788–94

Metcalfe, R., Powdthavee, N., Dolan, P., 2009, 'Destruction and distress: using a quasi-experiment to show the effects of the September 11 attacks on subjective well-being in the UK', Department of Economics and Related Studies, University of York, manuscript

Meyerowitz, B.E., Chaiken, S., 1987, 'The effect of message framing on breast self-examination attitudes, intentions, and behaviors', *Journal of Personality and Social Psychology*, 52, 500–10

Milgram, S., 1967, 'The small-world problem', *Psychology Today*, 1, 61–7

Milgram, S., 1974, *Obedience to Authority: an experimental view*, Tavistock Publishing

Miller, R.L., 1994, *Economics Today*, HarperCollins, London

Myers, D.G., 1993, *The Pursuit of Happiness: Who is happy, and Why?*, Harper Paperbacks

Ng, Y-K., 1997, 'A case for happiness, cardinalism, and interpersonal comparability', *Economic Journal*, 107(445), 1848–58

Okun, M.A., George, L.K., 1984, 'Physician- and self-ratings of health, neuroticism, and subjective well-being among men and women', *Personality and Individual Differences*, 5, 533–9

Oliver, J., 2007, *Affluenza*, Vermillion

Oreopoulos, P., 2007, 'Do dropouts drop out too soon? Wealth, health and happiness from compulsory schooling', *Journal of Public Economics*, 91, 2213–29

Ostir, G.V., Markides, K.S., Black, S.A., Goodwin, J.S., 2001, 'The association between emotional well-being and the incidence of stroke in older adults', *Psychosomatic Medicine*, 63, 210–15

Oswald, A.J., 1979, 'Wage determination in an economy with many trade unions', *Oxford Economic Papers*, 31, 369–85

Oswald, A.J., 1983, 'Altruism, jealousy and the theory of optimal non-linear taxation', *Journal of Public Economics*, 20, 77–88

Oswald, A.J., 2003, 'How much do external factors affect well-being? A way to use "happiness economics" to decide', *The Psychologist*, 16, 140–1

Oswald, A.J., 2006, 'What is a happiness equation?', Department of Economics, University of Warwick, manuscript

Oswald, A.J., Powdthavee, N., 2007, 'Obesity, unhappiness, and the challenge of affluence: theory and evidence', *Economic Journal*, 117, F441–54

Oswald, A.J., Powdthavee, N., 2008a, 'Death, happiness, and the calculation of compensatory damages', *Journal of Legal Studies*, 37(S2), S217–52

Oswald, A.J., Powdthavee, N., 2008b, 'Does happiness adapt? A longitudinal study of disability with implications for economists and judges', *Journal of Public Economics*, 92, 1061–77

Oswald, A.J., Powdthavee, N., 2010, 'Daughters and leftwing voting', *Review of Economics and Statistics*, 92(2), 213–27

Oswald, A.J., Proto, E., Sgroi, D., 2009, 'Happiness and productivity', Department of Economics, University of Warwick, manuscript

Oswald, A.J., Winkelmann, R., Powdthavee, N., 2010, 'Happiness and lottery wins in longitudinal data', University of Warwick, working paper

Oswald, A.J., Wu, S., 2010, 'Objective confirmation of subjective measures of human well-being: evidence from the USA', *Science*, 327, 576–9

Parducci, A., 1965, 'Category judgment: a range-frequency theory', *Psychological Review*, 72, 407–18

Paluck, E.L., 2009, 'Reducing intergroup prejudice and conflict using the media: a field experiment in Rwanda', *Journal of Personality and Social Psychology*, 96, 574–87

Peasgood, T., 2007, 'Does talking to our neighbours enhance satisfaction with life?', Imperial College London, manuscript

Persico, N., Postlewaite, A., and Silverman, D., 2004, 'The effect of adolescent experience and labour market outcomes: the case of height', *Journal of Political Economy*, 112(5), 1019–53

Post, F., 1996, 'Verbal creativity, depression and alcoholism: an investigation of one hundred American and British writers', *British Journal of Psychiatry*, 168, 545–55

Powdthavee, N., 2005, 'Unhappiness and crime: evidence from South Africa', *Economica*, 72, 531–47

Powdthavee, N., 2007a, 'Happiness and the standard of living: the case of South Africa', in L. Bruni, L. Porta (eds), *Handbook on the Economics of Happiness*, Edward Elgar, pp. 447–86

Powdthavee, N., 2007b, 'Are there psychological variations in the psychological cost of unemployment in South Africa?', *Social Indicators Research*, 80, 629–50

Powdthavee, N., 2008, 'Putting a price tag on friends, relatives, and neighbours: Using surveys of life satisfaction to value social relationships', *Journal of Socio-Economics*, 37, 1459–80

Powdthavee, N., 2009a, 'How important is rank to individual perception of economic standing? A within-community analysis', *Journal of Economic Inequality*, 7(3), 225–48

Powdthavee, N., 2009b, 'Does education reduce blood pressure? Estimating the biomarker effect of compulsory schooling in England', Department of Economics and Related Studies, University of York, working paper

Powdthavee, N., 2009c, 'Jobless, friendless, and broke: What happens to different areas of life before and after unemployment?', University of York, manuscript

Powdthavee, N., 2009d, 'Think having children will make you happy?', *Psychologist*, 22, 308–11

Powdthavee, N., 2009e, 'I can't smile without you: spousal correlation in life satisfaction', *Journal of Economic Psychology*, 30, 675–89

Powdthavee, N., 2010a, 'Causal analysis in happiness research', *Chulalongkorn Journal of Economics*, forthcoming

Powdthavee, N., 2010b, 'How much does money really matter? Estimating the causal effect of income on happiness', *Empirical Economics*, forthcoming

Powdthavee, N., Oswald, A.J., Wu, S., 2010, 'The effects of daughters on health choices and risky behaviours', University of York, manuscript

Powdthavee, N., Vignoles, A., 2008, 'Mental health of parents and life satisfaction of children: a within-family analysis of intergenerational transmission of well-being', *Social Indicators Research*, 88, 397–422

Priesner, S., 2004, 'Gross National Happiness: Bhutan's vision of development and its challenges', in P.N. Mukherji, C. Sengupta (eds), *Indigeneity and Universality in Social Science: A South Asian Response*, Sage, pp. 212–32

Prosecutor vs. Nahimana, Barayagwiza, and Ngeze, 2003, p. 29

Putnam, R.D., 2001, *Bowling Alone: the Collapse and Revival of American Community*, Simon & Schuster

Quattrone, G., Tversky, A., 1988, 'Contrasting rational and psychological analyses of political choices', *American Political Science Review*, 82, 719–36

Rayo, L., Becker, G.S., 2007, 'Evolutionary efficiency and happiness', *Journal of Political Economy*, 115, 302–37

Redelmeier, D., Kahneman, D., 1996, 'Patients' memories of painful medical treatments: Real-time and retrospective evaluations of two minimally invasive procedures', *Pain*, 66(1), 3–8

Riis, J., Lowenstein, G., Baron, J., Jepson, C., Fagerlin, A., Ubel, P.A., 2005, 'Ignorance of hedonic adaptation to hemodialysis: A study using ecological momentary assessment', *Journal of Experimental Psychology*, 134, 3–9

Robbins, L.C., 1938, 'Interpersonal Comparisons of Utility: A Comment', *Economic Journal*, 48, 635–41

Sales, S.M., House, J., 1971, 'Job dissatisfaction as a possible risk factor in coronary heart disease', *Journal of Chronic Diseases*, 23, 861–73

Samuelson, W., Zeckhauser, R.J., 1988, 'Status quo bias in decision making', *Journal of Risk and Uncertainty*, 1, 7–59

Sandvitz, E., Diener, E., Seidlitz, L., 1993, 'Subjective well-being: The convergence and stability of self and non self report measures', *Journal of Personality*, 61(3), 317–42

Sanna, L.J., Turley, K.J., Mark, M.M., 1996, 'Expected evaluation, goals, and performance: moods as input', *Journal of Personality and Social Psychology*, 22, 323–35

Schkade, D.A., Kahneman, D., 1998, 'Does living in California make people happy? A focusing illusion in judgements of life satisfaction', *Psychological Science*, 9, 340–6

Scott, J., 2000, 'Rational Choice Theory', in G. Browning, A. Halchi., F. Webster (eds), *Understanding Contemporary Society: Theories of the Present*, Sage Publications

Selvin, S., 1975, 'On the Monty Hall problem', *American Statistician*, 29, 134

Shedler, J., Mayman, M., Manis, M., 1993, 'The illusion of mental health', *American Psychologist*, 48(11), 1117–31

Simon, H.A., 1982, *Models of Bounded Rationality: Empirically Grounded Economic Reason*, MIT Press

Sloane, P.J., Williams, H., 2000, 'Job satisfaction, comparison earnings, and gender', *Labour*, 14, 473–501

Smith, T.W., 2007, 'Job satisfaction in the United States', NORC/University of Chicago, manuscript

Staw, B.M., Sutton, R.I., Pelled, L.H., 1994, 'Employee positive emotion and favourable outcomes at the workplace', *Organizational Science*, 5, 51–71

Steele, G.R., 2006, 'Richard Layard's *Happiness*: worn philosophy, weak psychology, wrong method and just plain bad economics', *Political Quarterly*, 77, 485–92

Steptoe, A., Wardle, J., 2005, 'Positive affect and biological function in everyday life', *Neurobiology of Ageing*, 26, S108–12

Stevenson, B., Wolfers, J., 2010, 'The paradox of declining female happiness', *American Economic Journal: Economic Policy*, forthcoming

Stutzer, A., 2004, 'The role of income aspirations in individual happiness', *Journal of Economic Behavior and Organization*, 54, 89–109

Stutzer, A., Frey, B., 2008, 'Stress that doesn't pay: the commuting paradox', *Scandinavian Journal of Economics*, 110, 339–66

Sunstein, C., 2003, 'Libertarian paternalism is not an oxymoron', *The University of Chicago Law Review*, 70, 1159–1202

Taylor, D.H., Hassellblad, V., Henley, S.J., Thun, M.J., Sloan, F.A., 2002, 'Benefits of smoking cessation for longevity', *American Journal of Public Health*, 92(6), 990–96

Thaler, R.H., 1980, 'Toward a positive theory of consumer choice', *Journal of Economic Behavior and Organization*, 1, 39–60

Thaler, R.H., Benartzi, S., 2004, 'Save More Tomorrow™: using behavioural economics to increase employee saving', *Journal of Political Economy*, 112, S164–87

Thaler, R.H., Sunstein, C.R., 2003, 'Libertarian paternalism', *American Economic Review*, 93, 175–9

Thaler, R.H., Sunstein, C.R., 2008, *Nudge: Improving Decisions about Health, Wealth and Happiness*, Penguin

Thoits, P.A., Hewitt, L.N., 2001, 'Volunteer work and well-being', *Journal of Health and Social Behavior*, 42, 115–31

Thoresen, C.J., Kaplan, S.A., Barsky, A.P., Warren, C.R., de Chermont, K., 2003, 'The affective underpinnings of job perceptions and attitudes: a meta-analytic review and integration', *Psychological Bulletin*, 129, 914–45

Tversky, A., Kahneman, D., 1981, 'The framing of decisions and the psychology of choice', *Science*, 211, 453–8

Tversky, A., Kahneman, D., 1986, 'Rational choice and the framing of decisions', *Journal of Business*, 59, S251–78

Tversky, A., Kahneman, D., 1991, 'Loss aversion and risky choice: a reference dependent model', *Quarterly Journal of Economics*, 106, 1039–61

Van Praag, B.M.S., 1991, 'Ordinal and cardinal utility: an integration of the two dimensions of the welfare concept', *Journal of Econometrics*, 50, 69–89

Van Praag, B.M.S., 2004, 'Using happiness surveys to value intangibles: the case of airport noise', *Economic Journal*, 115, 224–46

Veenhoven, R., 2000, 'Freedom and happiness: a comparative study in forty-four nations in the early 1990s', in E. Diener, E.M. Suh (eds), *Culture and Subjective Well-Being*, MIT Press, pp. 257–88

Welsch, H., 2009, 'Implications of happiness research for environmental economics', *Ecological Economics*, 68, 2735–42

White, M.P., Dolan, P., 2009, 'Accounting for the richness of daily activities', *Psychological Science*, 20, 1000–08

Wilson, T.D., 2002, *Strangers to Ourselves: Discovering the adaptive unconscious*, Harvard University Press, Cambridge MA

Wilson, T.D., Gilbert, D.T., 2008, 'Explaining away: a model of affective adaptation', *Perspectives on Psychological Science*, 3, 370–86

Wilson, T.D., Wheatley, T.P., Meyers, J.M., Gilbert, D.T., Axsom, D., 2000, 'Focalism: A source of durability bias in affective forecasting', *Journal of Personality and Social Psychology*, 78, 821–36

Winkelmann, R., Winkelmann, L., 1998, 'Why are the unemployed so unhappy? Evidence from panel data', *Economica*, 65, 1–16

Wolfers, J., Stevenson, B., 2008, 'Economic growth and subjective well-being: reassessing the Easterlin Paradox', *Brookings Paper on Economic Activity*, 1, 1–87

Wooldridge, J., 2002, *Econometric Analysis of Cross-section and Panel Data*, MIT Press

Wortman, C., Coates, D., 1985, 'Obituary: Philip Brickman (1943–1982)', *American Psychologist*, 40, 1051–2

Zimmerman, A., Easterlin, R.A., 2006, 'Happily ever after? Cohabitation, marriage, divorce, and happiness in Germany', *Population and Development Review*, 32, 511–28

Acknowledgements

There are many people to whom I wish to express my gratitude. My literary agent, Curtis Russell, has been an unfailing provider of support throughout the completion of this book, and I'd like to thank him personally for constantly reminding me that I really have an interesting story to tell. I'd also like to thank my editor at Icon Books, Duncan Heath, who did excellent and meticulous editorial work on the manuscript, as well as Simon Flynn, Andrew Furlow and the rest of the team at Icon. Thank you ever so much for taking a chance on me.

I would also like to offer my indebted thanks to my colleagues and friends with whom I have enjoyed countless discussions about my beloved subject – happiness. Andrew Oswald, my mentor and friend, deserves the most credit for taking me under his wing. He didn't have to, and for that I am for ever thankful. To his partner, Amanda Goodall, I would like to offer my continued appreciation and affection for her advice and general enthusiasm throughout my early career in academia. To Richard Easterlin and Mathew White, I wish to express my gratitude for taking time to read the manuscript and for giving top-notch comments. To *Ajarn* Gordon Bailey, Leslie Godfrey, Daniel Gilbert, Claudia Senik, Nicholas Christakis, James Fowler, Paul Frijters, Robert Metcalfe, Paul Dolan, Tess Peasgood, Richard Layard, Daniel Kahneman, Anna Vignoles, Ricardo Sabates, Geeta Kingdon, Robin Naylor, Erzo Luttmer, Mauro Bambi, Michalis Drouvelis, Richard Cookson, Carol Graham, Bruno Frey, Alois Stutzer, Anke Plagnol, Andrew Clark, Ed Diener, Richard E. Lucas, Yannis Georgellis, Andrew Postlewaite, Silvia Pezzini, Nicola Persico, Ian and Marjory Sinclair, Somkiat Tangkitvanich, Ammar Siamwalla, and John

Hey, I would like to offer my deepest appreciation for their helpful insights and suggestions over the years.

There are also many people here at the University of York whom I wish to thank. To P'Yui, Yim, Punn, and Nook, thank you so much for treating me to hot Thai food whenever I had nothing left over in my fridge. To Nuch and Auu, thank you for keeping me company at the department whenever I had to stay in late to complete this book. Thank you Warn, Ong, Tum, Kwang, Kung, Chew, P'Yo, Tee+, Kook, Pink, Vow, Note, Ben, Pook, P'Pong, Pu, Tuk, Weng, Fred, Jao, Lyn, Chai, Nine, Note, Steffen, Nina, Champ, Matthias, and many others who have either helped me pick the right cover for this book or have been enthusiastic about the book itself. To Richard and Charlotte Partridge, and Robert and Sasha Winzar, thank you for continuing to be my best friends and my number one fans. I would also like to thank my parents, Somchai and Daranee Powdthavee, for not doubting that their son could actually write a book. And to my grandmothers, thank you for being the good and strong role models that you are.

And finally, to my Nateecha, you were there when I first stumbled into the weird and wonderful world of happiness research. And as strange as that world was to you at the time, you chose to stay and keep me warm. For that, I am eternally grateful. You are, and forever will be, my be-all and end-all.

INDEX